the canine chef cookbook

"Tested & Approved by Kirby the Dorkie"

Debby Martin

Copyright © 2015 by Debby Martin

the canine chef cookbook
by Debby Martin

Printed in the United States of America.

ISBN 9781498439985

All rights reserved solely by the author. The author guarantees all contents are original and do not infringe upon the legal rights of any other person or work. No part of this book may be reproduced in any form without the permission of the author. The views expressed in this book are not necessarily those of the publisher.

Disclaimer: This publication is to provide information to help you prepare nutritious, homemade treats and meals for your dog(s). It is not intended to diagnose, cure, or prevent disease or illness or replace the expert care and specific nutritional advice provided by your veterinarian.

Even though I have done extensive research, you should always seek the advice of your veterinarian before changing your dog's dietary healthcare or adding any ingredients to your dog's food especially when underlying health conditions may exist. Many medical conditions require specific foods or prohibit specific foods.

Nutrition is just one part of a total holistic approach to your dog's health. To find a holistic veterinarian, please visit the American Holistic Veterinary Medical Association online at www.ahvma.org.

KitchenAid® is a trademark of the Whirlpool Corporation.

www.xulonpress.com

table of contents

Acknowledgements vii
Foreword ix
Introduction xi
Kirby The Dorkie xiii

Wholesome Canine Nutrition 15
    Healthy Ingredients 17
    Harmful Ingredients 25
    Safe Herbs & Spices 29
    Safe Flours. 35
    The Incredible Egg 37
    Make It Egg Free 38
    Garlic Is Good 39
    Safe Food Colors 41
    Soak Those Grains 43
    Homemade Meals 45
    Portion Control 47

The Recipes 49
    Baked Treats 51
    Baked Grain Free Treats 101
    Frostings for Special Occasions 116
    No Bake Treats 121
    Frozen Treats 141
    Fillings for Kongs or Bones 155
    Dehydrated Treats 157
    Meals 179
    Grain Free Meals 207
    Toppers and Side Dishes 247
    Make Your Own Chicken Stock 257
    Make Your Own Bone Broth 258

The Pantry 261
    Tips & Tricks. 263
    Dealing with Dough 266
    Is It Still Good? 268
    Stocking the Canine Pantry 270
    Tools in the Kitchen 271
    Conversion Charts 273
    BONUS: The Soap of Royalty Dog Shampoo 277

Resources 279
Ingredient Index 281

acknowledgements

For all the furry foodies hungry for a tempting morsel filled with flavor and nutrition.

For all who love their furkids in the hope that they may experience the joy of making healthy meals and treats in their own kitchens.

My soul belongs to God who has filled me with a thirst for knowledge bringing a joy in the kitchen while creating these recipes. Without Him, I would truly be lost.

My heart belongs to Kirby who is my muse, my loyal side kick, my angel in fur. This little sous chef dearly loves good food and, as a picky connoisseur, ever pushes me to strive for the healthiest combinations of flavor to satisfy his taste tests.

A special thank you to my family, friends, and fans who have supported this endeavor. Without your questions and interest this journey would have meant so much less. Your devotion and loyalty are appreciated more than you will ever know.

Last but not least, thank you to everyone who purchases our cookbook because you are fulfilling my dream of feeding your beloved furkids the wholesome ingredients God has provided for vital health and longevity. What goes in really does shine out.

www.kirbythedorkie.com

This is where you'll find new recipes, DIY projects, product reviews, and giveaways!

www.facebook.com/KirbytheDorkie

This is where Kirby interacts with his fans.

www.pinterest.com/KirbytheDorkie

foreword

I have known Kirby and his mama since he was a puppy. Kirby has been coming to my clinic for his necessary check-ups, vaccinations and preventatives for the past six years. He is a very healthy, happy and active dog. He maintains his weight and has healthy skin and coat. Kirby sees us most frequently for nail trims. Unfortunately, he dislikes these nail trims, so I don't think I am one of his favorite people.

Proper nutrition is the cornerstone in maximizing health, performance, longevity, and disease prevention. Nutrition touches all aspects of your pet's health and is the key to the prevention and management of many diseases. Specific diets and certain supplements alone can be used to prevent and treat many ailments we see on a daily basis at the clinic. It is important to remember that improper diet is the root cause of several disorders by which pets are affected.

Like many pet guardians, Ms. Martin is concerned about additives and possible contaminants found in commercial pet foods. She chooses to make the majority of Kirby's meals at home from scratch. As long as the recipes are balanced and varied with the right amounts and types of proteins, carbohydrates and fats, homemade meals can be healthy and preferred by pets. While most dogs do fine on commercial kibble, some have intolerances and sensitivities to additives, preservatives, and certain proteins and grains. The majority of human food products have these same potentially dangerous additives in them. When thinking about your own health, you monitor your food and make decisions by reading food labels, buying fresh and organic, or making meals from known ingredients. Your pet will benefit from the same decisions and use of healthy diverse ingredients.

Be sure to provide your pet with a good quality multivitamin made specifically for his or her species, and if he is used to a specific diet, gradually change and introduce new foods over 3 to 7 days. If any specific food seems to upset his digestive tract, discontinue that food and try another. Remember treats are small snacks with calories that add up and work with your veterinarian if your pet has any underlying health issues. There are a lot of nutritious ingredients out there from which to choose. This cookbook contains a lot of wholesome recipes tested and approved by Kirby and many of our shelter dogs. Some of them sound good enough to try myself!

Rita Morris, DVM

Choctaw Animal Clinic

Choctaw County Animal Shelter

http://www.facebook.com/choctawanimalclinic

introduction

When Kirby came into my life I gladly purchased what I thought was the healthiest dog food and treats. Over time I became aware of the difference between bad, good, and exceptional dog foods. I then began preparing the majority of his meals using healthy, wholesome ingredients from my local grocery store. Next, I began creating his treats and soon discovered I was in love with the whole process.

Extensive research has led me to discover just what his body does and doesn't need to live a long, active and healthy life. I love discovering new ingredients that are dog friendly and blending just the right amount of each to create something that makes him drool. Through lots of trial and error, some creations are perfect the first time, some creations require tweaking, and sadly, some creations never make it past the nose test much less the taste test. A recipe must meet my strict criteria and pass Kirby's taste test before it can be considered a keeper.

These are the answers to some of the questions I have been asked over the years.

Why do I prepare the majority of Kirby's meals and treats? The dog food recalls, the dog treat recalls, and the fact that I was slowly poisoning Kirby with subpar, even dangerous, commercial dog food before I knew what I know now has led me to take great care as to what goes into his body for optimal nutrition and longevity of life. Not only is Kirby thriving with a beautiful coat, bright eyes and boundless energy, I have seen our foster dogs transform from the scraggly, malnourished states in which they arrived to healthy, energetic animals when they left for their forever homes.

Why do I follow a rotation diet to provide a variety in Kirby's diet? Varying wholesome real foods on a regular basis lessens the chance of developing food allergies many dogs develop to certain proteins or grains due to repeatedly eating the same foods over and over again. Also, rotating meat and vegetables exposes him to a healthier range of nutrient sources and inhibits the boredom factor. Imagine only eating a hamburger and fries with ice cream for dessert every day. Not only would that be unhealthy, just think of all the flavors and nutrients your body and taste buds are missing out on. Just as we humans have cravings, so do dogs. I know Kirby's favorite flavors and what he doesn't like. For example, he greatly dislikes carrots which are very nutritious and low fat. An easy remedy? Hide the chopped carrots in a meal or treat.

Warning: New foods should be introduced gradually to allow the appropriate gut flora to develop. If your dog is not used to a dietary variety, then patience is required to strengthen his digestive system. Dogs who are accustomed to eating a monotonous diet may have a weakened system that may take time to allow them to readily digest fresh food. A trick I've learned with new fosters is to add a teaspoon or two of pure pumpkin to their meals to help their bodies adjust. This amazing ingredient has the ability to either correct any bouts of diarrhea or relieve constipation.

Why do I use portion control when feeding Kirby? Free feeding is easier but then I have no way of knowing how much he has eaten or not eaten if he is ill. Portion control provides the information I need to oversee his well-being. Wondering how much to feed your pup on a daily basis? Refer to my Portion Control to understand and determine the proper daily portion your dog needs.

Why do I not worry about achieving proper nutritional balance? I raised two healthy children and never worried about counting or measuring vitamins or minerals. Common sense told me they were receiving what their bodies needed from the variety of healthy foods they consumed every day. They also took a daily multivitamin to ensure they received any low or missing nutrients. Kirby is provided a wide variety of healthy appropriate foods and takes a daily multivitamin. In a nutshell I believe the basic principles of sensible eating should apply to our pets as well.

For those concerned about proper nutritional proportions, they generally run 25 – 60 percent meat, 30 percent carbohydrates (grain or sweet potato) and 20-40 percent vegetables. A multi vitamin plus calcium are recommended.

Why do I only allow Kirby to eat a small amount of dry kibble on a daily basis? The natural diet of dogs is made up of 70 percent water which means moisture content is missing in a mainly dry food diet. Kibble is just too dry to be considered healthy as it requires the dog's body to provide sufficient moisture to reconstitute the food in their digestive tract. Over time this becomes stressful to multiple organs, especially the kidneys.

kirby the dorkie

Thus far I've been blessed with three heart dogs, that special dog that just gets you. A unique bond that can't be explained. Chevas was there when I was a child and Sugar was there when I had children. Heartbroken, it would be seven dogless years before I would meet my next heart dog.

I was puppy sitting an adorable four month old Dorkie named Tucker for my daughter who ended up with him after someone had purchased him for his wife who it turned out did not want a dog. She was trying to find him a home, so seeing how he completely stole my heart, I kept him. He lived with me until the age of seven months when he was struck by a car. I still see it as if it just happened. I couldn't stop the car, I couldn't stop Tucker. I heard his yelp of pain as I saw the front fender hit his head. The car never stopped even though I was screaming and crying and running towards them. I watched the light leave his eyes as I held him in my arms for the last time. I knew it was my fault but it was easier to be angry at God. He could have saved him. He could have prevented it from ever happening. We buried sweet Tucker in his bed with his blanket and favorite toys.

Friends pushed me to get another dog saying I had waited far too long since Sugar passed. So I prayed, except I prayed in an angry sort of way only God would understand. I made my demands knowing it wasn't possible. First, it had to be a Dorkie. Second, it had to be a male. Third, it had to have the black and tan markings Tucker had. Fourth, it had to be what I could afford. God laughed as He easily checked off each demand.

I halfheartedly began searching the internet discovering there were only a few Dorkie breeders across the country. Even if I could afford one there would also be the additional cost of flying the poor creature to Mississippi. I felt an unexpected glimmer of hope when I came across an ad for Dorkie puppies in Senatobia, Mississippi, which was just a few hours away. A family had let their two dogs (an AKC Yorkie and a CKC F1 Dorkie) breed and had a litter due soon. They weren't hopeful since the only other litter had produced three girls. But they promised to keep me updated. *Close to home and only $250*

January 9, 2009. Just another ordinary day but for the fact my little Kirby (a whopping 3 ounces) was born. Three boys and a girl. One male was chocolate brown but two had the black and tan markings. When they were three weeks old a friend and I decided to take a drive to visit. *Not one but two males with the black and tan markings.*

We spent a few hours playing with the pups. The first one (later named Reese by his adoptive mom) was such a pretty boy with long hair. He was a bundle of energy, just wouldn't be still for a second. The other little guy was smaller and had shorter hair. He was playful but he loved to snuggle. Those dark brown eyes looked into mine and stole my heart that very day. With a magic marker he was marked as mine. Only three weeks until I could take him home!

During those weeks of waiting I did what every normal pet parent-to-be does. I went shopping… a fluffy dog bed, a dog's teddy bear, actually two, dog dishes, collar, leash, dog food, treats, a book on puppies, the usual stuff. I started a list of names adding and then marking off until I was down to two names I really liked that were daughter approved. Kirby or Kingston.

Adoption Day! I went a day earlier just to be sure because a lady from Georgia was picking out her puppy on Saturday. My daughter really liked the other boy (fluffiest was the word she used) but the little snuggly one pulled at my heartstrings. My choice had been made so, without hesitation, I adopted Kirby and brought him home.

Sir Kirby Kingston Martin of Mississippi is his CKC registered name so on paper Kirby is a very important little guy! To us he's just Kirby or Kirby Bear or Boo Bear or Rug Rat or Sweet Boy or Pretty boy! He has gotten me through some dark days with his silly antics and unconditional love making me a better person along the way. His fearlessness inspires me to take chances while his endless happiness teaches me to appreciate what each new day brings. A gift from God who makes me smile as he touches the hearts of every human and foster dog he meets.

A Note: Tucker looked more Dachshund with a very short coat and long floppy ears. Kirby looked like him as a pup but over time grew a Yorkie coat with ears that stand halfway up and halfway down. Both have the long back and muzzle with the muscular Dachshund body. God knew what He was doing. I wanted my Tucker but Kirby grabbed hold of my heart with both paws in his own unique way. *Answered prayer.*

AKC – American Kennel Club

CKC – Continental Kennel Club

Dorkie F1 – 1st generation offspring from a pure bred Yorkshire Terrier and a pure bred Dachshund.

Dorkie F1b – 2nd generation offspring from a pure bred Yorkshire Terrier or a pure bred Dachshund and an F1 Dorkie.

wholesome canine nutrition

healthy ingredients

These are the ingredients deemed to be safe and beneficial by holistic veterinarians and canine nutritional experts which I use in Kirby's recipes. If any make you feel uncomfortable, discuss it with your veterinarian or simply omit it from the recipe.

Almond milk is lactose, dairy, soy, gluten, egg, saturated fat, MSG and peanut free. It is derived from almonds which are rich in vitamin E antioxidants, vitamins A and D, and has as much calcium as regular milk.

Anchovies are high in omega-3 fatty acids, protein, niacin, and selenium and very low in calories. Because they're small fish that are low on the food chain, they're unlikely to harbor high levels of mercury, PCB's, dioxins, or other contaminants. *Soak the anchovies in milk for 10-15 minutes to remove the majority of salt.*

Apples are a good source of dietary fiber and vitamin C which can help hip dysplasia, a common ailment in large purebred dogs while low in saturated fat and sodium. Apples help calm the digestive system and have the ability to help the body absorb calcium and iron from other foods. *Beware of apple seeds which contain amygdalin, a form of cyanide that prevents the blood from carrying oxygen throughout the body. If your dog has kidney trouble don't give him apples because they contain calcium and phosphorous which can greatly aggravate the problem.*

Avocados are an excellent source of fiber, potassium (containing 60% more than bananas), vitamin K, vitamin B9, vitamin B6, vitamin B5 vitamin C, and vitamin E, and research suggests this fruit can lower cholesterol levels, reduce the risk of diabetes, promote lower body weight, and prevent cancer. Avocados have had a bad rap for years as rumors abounded to its toxicity for dogs. *It is the pit or seed, skin and leaves which contain an oil-soluble toxin called persin which can be deadly for birds, rabbits, horses, and cattle.* Holistic vets agree the meat of the avocado is not only safe but has healthy benefits for dogs. Kirby has been eating avocados since a pup with no adverse reactions. *Too much can cause vomiting and diarrhea, so exercise caution and limit the intake.*

Bacon is a cured meat prepared from pig which is cured using large quantities of salt. *So while this fatty meat isn't considered a healthy ingredient it can be used sparingly so I've added it to the list. Bacon made from turkey is a healthier option.*

Bananas have vitamin B6 and C, potassium, and adds natural acidophilus bacteria to the bowels in small amounts.

Barley is a healthy high fiber, high protein whole grain boasting numerous health benefits. When cooked, barley has a chewy texture and nutty flavor similar to brown rice. This grain's soluble fiber reduces the risk of heart disease and can lower cholesterol. With less than one gram of fat per serving, barley is a virtually fat free, cholesterol free food. An excellent choice for specialized obesity and diabetic pet diets due to its unique nutritional make-up, modest amounts of slowly digested starch and the soluble fiber B-glucan. Pearled barley is more digestible than whole or cracked barley.

Beans are very high in protein, nonfat, high in fiber and low in soluble carbs. They help regulate blood sugar levels, one of the leading causes of insulin resistance and diabetes in dogs. In addition, these rich sources of proteins and minerals boost the immune system and help burn fat. Just about every type of bean is acceptable; pinto, white, northern, black, red, refried, chickpeas, and black eyed peas. Contrary to belief, the possibility of gas and flatulence if dogs are fed beans does not commonly occur.

Beef is an excellent source of high quality protein.

Beets are loaded with vitamins A, B1, B2, B6 and C. They are also an excellent source of calcium, magnesium, copper, phosphorus, sodium and iron. While the sweet beet root has some of the minerals in its greens to a lesser degree, it is also a remarkable source of choline, folic acid, iodine, manganese, organic sodium, potassium, fiber and carbohydrates in the form of natural digestible sugars.

Bison, also known as buffalo, has a sweeter and richer flavor than beef and nutritionally it has more protein and nutrients with fewer calories and less fat than beef, chicken or salmon. Bison is a dense meat that tends to satisfy more while eating less.

Blueberries have manganese, vitamins B6, C, K, and fiber. They are rich in vitamin A & C, potassium, fiber and various carotenoids which are valuable anti-oxidants.

Broths and stocks made from scratch provide a rich beef, chicken or fish flavor without the fats or dangerous seasonings which can be found in most commercial brands. It's full of minerals, including calcium, silicon, sulphur, magnesium and phosphorus. It supports the immune system, detoxes the liver, provides glucosamine to protect the joints, and helps maintain a healthy gut, especially for dogs with digestive issues

Brown Rice is an excellent source of complex carbohydrates, provides quick energy and is loaded with B vitamins and minerals. The bran layer is what makes the rice rich in fiber and requires a longer cooking time in order for it to become tender.

Buckwheat is a fruit seed related to rhubarb and sorrel making it a suitable substitute for those sensitive to wheat or other grains that contain protein glutens. It's a good source of fiber and magnesium, significantly lowers blood glucose and insulin responses, may be helpful in the management of diabetes, can help avoid gallstones, and protect against hormone-dependent cancers as well as heart disease.

Butter, unsalted, contains CLA which is a naturally occurring fat shown in rodent studies to help prevent cancer growth as well as lowering body fat percentage. It contains vitamin A, vitamin E and vitamin K2 which aids calcium metabolism of which a low intake has been associated with cardiovascular disease, cancer and osteoporosis. Additionally, butter contains short and medium chain fats which are metabolized differently from other fats leading to improved satiety and increased fat burning. *It does have a high calorie count so you may want to feed sparingly.*

Carob is low in fat and sodium, high in fiber, potassium, and calcium, and can improve digestion. It has a natural sweetness and contains very little fat, no caffeine and encourages the absorption of calcium. Even though carob looks like, smells like, and has a taste that is similar to chocolate, it does not contain theobromine, the part of chocolate that is toxic to dogs.

Carrots are high in vitamin A, rich in dietary fiber, antioxidants and minerals, low calorie, low fat, and a good natural source of beta carotene, an antioxidant essential for neutralizing free radicals.

Cheese is high in protein and calcium. Newer studies indicate cheese may actually re-mineralize your pet's teeth and reduce the acids that cause plaque and lead to cavities. Cheese also helps to protect an aging pet from osteoporosis.

Cherries contain powerful antioxidants called anthocyanins and nutrients such as beta carotene, vitamin C, potassium, magnesium, iron, fiber and folate. They are a blood builder, can assist with elimination, help remove toxic substances, help reduce inflammation due to arthritis, and reduce risk factors for heart disease. *No pits!*

Chicken is one of the best sources of lean proteins, various vitamins, minerals and all nine essential amino acids while low in fat and cholesterol. It has significant amounts of phosphorous and potassium and selenium. Iron and zinc content in dark meat is much higher than that in white meat.

Chicken Liver is an excellent source of high quality protein and a rich source of vitamins A, D and virtually all of the B vitamins.

Coconut is made up of a beneficial fatty acid chain called Lauric acid. When dogs synthesize Lauric acid it produces something called monoglyceride monolaurin which helps fight and destroy viruses and various pathogenic bacteria protecting from infection and boosting the immune system. It also contains albumin, a water-soluble protein found in many animal tissues and liquids that significantly assists in the formation of red blood cells. It elevates metabolism and boosts energy by helping to regulate the thyroid helping overweight dogs lose weight and helping sedentary dogs feel energetic. Other benefits of coconut include improved skin and coat, improved digestion, reduction in odor, and minimized allergic reactions. It can even help kill worm eggs and rid your pet of ear mites. Coconut is available in many forms - coconut flour, coconut milk, coconut oil, and coconut butter. The optimum amount for dogs is about 1 teaspoon daily per 10 pounds of body weight, or 1 tablespoon per 30 pounds of body weight.

Cranberries help normalize your pet's bladder health, aid in urinary tract health, contains echinacea which is believed to stimulate the immune system, flavonoids which may fend off cancer and inhibit tumor growth, and vitamin C. *Dogs may be given small amounts of cranberries but never large amounts which can cause diarrhea. Never give your dog cranberry juice which has a chemical that prevents bacteria from adhering to the wall of the bladder.*

Dried Kelp is the dried product from two families of seaweed. It is an excellent natural source of iodine and also provides beneficial fiber.

Duck is an excellent source of high quality protein and fatty acids. *It is a fatty meat so feed sparingly.*

Eggs contain all of the essential amino acids and are an excellent form of digestible protein containing riboflavin, selenium and are an excellent source of protein. *Raw egg whites contain avidin which binds to biotin (B vitamin) to make it unavailable to the pet so it is not recommended to feed pets raw eggs.*

Egg shells are a great calcium supplement for dogs fed a homemade diet. Adding calcium will balance the excess phosphorus found in red meat diets that don't include bone. You can use any kind of eggs (chicken, duck, etc.), but choose certified organic eggs from free-range, naturally fed birds. If the bird isn't supplied with proper nutrition the egg shells won't contain the needed nutrients. Eggshells contain calcium and micro-elements like magnesium, boron, copper, iron, manganese, molybdenum, sulphur, silicon and zinc, etc. In total there are 27 vital elements. The composition of an egg shell is very similar to that of bones and teeth. They must be ground to a fine powder in order for them to be digestible.

Gelatin has many benefits. In the wild carnivores naturally consume gelatin and its primary amino acid, glycine, in the skin, tendons and cartilage of their prey. It has anti-inflammatory and brain protective actions which are especially important during aging and when under stress. Glycine, the main amino acid in gelatin, protects against seizures and brain damage. The benefits of gelatin for dogs with arthritis may include reduced inflammation and reduced pain. However, gelatin is most beneficial if fed as a preventive to help healthy dogs avoid joint disease. Plain, unflavored gelatin is fat and cholesterol free and can be purchased at any grocery store. It can be sprinkled on the food once a day. Try mixing with chicken broth and cut into cubes for an easy dog treat.

Green Beans have lots of green chlorophyll, is fully digestible and packed with nutrients.

Herring is a source of protein and long chain Omega 3 fatty acids which are critical for healthy skin and coat, proper body function and enhanced learning of young puppies.

Honey contains vitamins A, B-complex, C, D, E, and K, plus calcium, phosphorus, magnesium, silicon, sulfur, potassium, manganese, copper, and iodine. It's a source of natural energy, a tonic for the nervous system and heart, immediately absorbed by the blood and inhibits the development of pathogenic bacteria in the digestive system. It increases absorption of calcium consumed at the same time, helps treat or prevent anemia, reduces arthritis pain, and works as a gentle laxative to help prevent constipation.

Holistic studies have shown dogs suffering from environmental allergies can greatly benefit from raw, local honey. One teaspoon for small dogs or one tablespoon for large dogs can help ease the symptoms of allergies by exposing your dog to a very low level of the substance causing an allergic reaction by developing immunity over time. It is important that the honey is raw and local to your area. When the body is safely exposed to those pollens on a very small level, the body can grow accustomed to the allergens and thus have little to no reaction.

Kale is a nutrient dense leafy green containing beta carotene, calcium, vitamin C, vitamin K, and lutein. It has anti-inflammatory properties, antioxidants and healthy flavonoids, and is believed to help prevent cancer.

Lamb is an excellent source of protein.

Liver (chicken, calf, beef, deer, and bison) is a nutrient rich organ meat that provides protein, fat, vitamin A, copper, iron, niacin, phosphorus and zinc. It provides many B vitamins, omega-3 and omega-6 fatty acids, and essential amino acids. Release any toxins stored in the liver by placing the thawed and drained liver in a container with about 2 tablespoons of apple cider vinegar and refrigerate overnight. *While liver offers many health benefits, it can also be harmful if your dog eats too much of it leading to a condition called hypervitaminosis A (overdose of vitamin A) so only feed up to three small servings a week. Symptoms of a vitamin A overdose can include bone deformity, bone spurs on the dog's legs or spine that cause him to limp, digestive upsets, muscle weakness, stiffness or weight loss.*

Maple syrup (pure) is a natural sweetener with over 54 antioxidants that can help delay or prevent diseases caused by free radicals such as cancer or diabetes. It's an excellent source of manganese, riboflavin, zinc, calcium, and potassium. It's used to treat hypoglycemia in Yorkies and there are studies using maple syrup to fight cancer in dogs.

Milk provides calcium, protein, B vitamins, vitamin A, and potassium. It can also protect from osteoporosis and colon cancer. *Many dogs are lactose intolerant so watch for signs such as abdominal pain, bloating, nausea, vomiting and diarrhea. Sometimes a dog will drink excess amounts of water when suffering from lactose intolerance since the diarrhea and vomiting can cause dehydration and consequent thirst. If concerned, or your dog is lactose intolerant, use lactose free milk.*

Molasses (Blackstrap) is a natural sweetener rich in B vitamins, calcium, magnesium, potassium and iron.

Oats contain healthy amounts of fiber, selenium (which fights cancer), B vitamins and iron and are an excellent source of highly digestible carbohydrates.

Olive oil is considered a healthful dietary oil because of its high content of monounsaturated fat (mainly oleic fatty acid) and polyphenols which are good for skin and coat health and as a treatment for constipation. *Most oils, if unopened and stored in a cool dark place, will still be good for up to two years. Light oils are delicate so use it within six months or a year at the most from date of harvest.*

Oranges are an excellent source of vitamin C, contain generous levels of folate (folic acid), potassium, and thiamin, as well as some calcium and magnesium. Their supply of flavonoids make them a valuable aid in strengthening the immune system, supporting connective tissues, and promoting overall good health. They have been shown to protect against cancer, and fight viral infections.

Peas are an excellent source of protein and fiber.

Peanut butter is high in protein, amino acids, polyunsaturated fatty acids, calcium, phosphorus and niacin. Peanuts are actually legumes, not nuts. Choose natural brands that contain 100% peanuts. *It can be fattening so feed peanut butter sparingly.*

Pears are an excellent source of pectin.

Potatoes provide vitamins B3 and B6, vitamin C, potassium, iron, copper and fiber. Significant quantities of manganese, molybdenum, chromium and selenium can be found just beneath the potato's skin. They are an anti-inflammatory (except in some arthritic conditions), as well as being able to neutralize body acids and benefit stomach ulcers. Potatoes calm and heal the digestive mucosa as well as work as an antispasmodic, diuretic and emollient. Its rich potassium content helps to eliminate uric acid. *Avoid the stems, shoots and green parts of the skin which are toxic to dogs.*

Pumpkin is packed with large quantities of vitamin A for resistance to infections, improve night vision and keep the body's membranes healthy, potassium for good blood pressure, iron for healthy blood, and roughage to help digestion. Pumpkin has been documented to regulate both constipation and diarrhea in dogs. *Only use fresh pumpkin or canned pumpkin, never pumpkin pie mix which has sugar and other harmful ingredients.*

Quinoa (keen-wa) which has a mild, nutty flavor and a light, fluffy texture similar to couscous is often classified as a whole grain but is a seed from a vegetable related to swiss chard, spinach and beets. It's gluten free, high in fiber and high quality protein, iron and potassium. One half cup of quinoa has 14 grams of protein and 6 grams of fiber.

Rye Flour is very low in gluten and contains more protein, phosphorus, iron, potassium and B vitamins than whole wheat.

Safflower oil, which is flavorless and colorless, is a good source of vitamins E and K, contains omega 6 fatty acids, and may help moisturize your dog's skin.

Salmon is an excellent source of high quality protein, calcium, phosphorous and long chain omega 3 fatty acids, which are critical for healthy skin, coat and proper body function.

Salmon oil is high in omega 3 fatty acids, specifically EPA and DHA.

Sardines are full of omega-3 fatty acids which help prevent cancer, reduce inflammation, keep the immune system strong, and help brain development. They also contain Coenzyme Q10 which supports a healthy heart and circulation, and prevent dental disease. One small sardine contains 25 calories and 175 mg of omega-3 fatty acids, a good dose for a dog who weighs 20 pounds or less. Sardines are a small fish so they don't have time to pick up heavy metals in their short lives.

Spelt flour which has a mild nutty flavor is naturally high in fiber, contains significantly more protein than wheat, is also higher in B complex vitamins, and both simple and complex carbohydrates. Another important benefit is that those who are gluten sensitive have been able to include spelt based foods in their diets.

Spinach is rich in vitamins and minerals. It's concentrated in health-promoting phytonutrients such as carotenoids and flavonoids to provide powerful antioxidant protection against inflammatory problems, oxidative stress-related problems, cardiovascular problems, bone problems, and cancers at the same time. The vitamin K provided by spinach is important for maintaining bone health. Vitamin K1 helps prevent excessive activation of osteoclasts, the cells that break down bone. Additionally, friendly bacteria in the intestines convert vitamin K1 into vitamin K2, which activates osteocalcin, the major non-collagen protein in bone. Osteocalcin anchors calcium molecules inside of the bone. Spinach is also an excellent source of other bone-supportive nutrients including calcium and magnesium.

Squash is an excellent source of beta carotene, vitamin C and potassium.

Sweet Potatoes and Yams are low in sodium and very low in saturated fat and cholesterol, a good source of dietary fiber, vitamin B6, potassium, vitamin A, vitamin C and manganese. They have even been known to help regulate blood sugar levels in diabetics. *Raw sweet potatoes contain a substance that inhibits trypsin, a natural enzyme necessary for the pancreas to digest proteins.*

Tomatoes contain high levels of vitamin C, vitamin A, and the powerful antioxidant lycopene which was proven to lower the risk of cancer and degenerative diseases. *Beware that dogs cannot eat the green unripe fruits, leaves, or stem which contain tropane and atropine alkaloids which are highly poisonous to dogs. Excessive drooling, vomiting, diarrhea or constipation are signs of tomato toxicity. The toxins will cause tremors, muscle weakness and breathing difficulties which can lead to coma and death.*

Tuna, which is low in fat and calories, is packed with lean protein, vitamins B and D, and omega-3 fatty acids known to relieve joint pain, protect the heart, promote brain health and boost the immune system.

Turkey has more protein per gram than both chicken and beef while remaining lower in fat and cholesterol than other meats. It also delivers vitamins and minerals, especially niacin which facilitates the conversion of food into available energy, and vitamin B6 which is important for the health of the nervous system. Turkey also has selenium which is essential for proper thyroid and immune function.

Turnip greens are an excellent source of vitamin K, vitamin C, carotenoids, most B vitamins, fiber and manganese. They are also a good source of calcium, copper, potassium, magnesium and phosphorus, and provide a complement of antioxidants.

Venison (deer) is an excellent source of protein, while, unlike most meats, it tends to be fairly low in fat, especially saturated fat. It's a good source of iron, vitamin B12, vitamin B6, riboflavin, and niacin.

Whitefish (cod, haddock, sea bass, pollack, coley, hake, whiting, plaice, sole, John Dory, halibut, flounder and turbot) is an excellent source of high quality protein, calcium, phosphorous and long chain omega 6 fatty acids, which are critical for healthy skin, coat and body function.

Yogurt provides probiotics promoting healthy digestion, eliminating unhealthy bacteria and providing healthy bacteria, it also fights such nasty germs as Salmonella typhimurium and Staphyloccus aureus.

harmful ingredients

This is the list of what NOT to feed your dog. If you think your dog has consumed something toxic call your veterinarian or the ASCPA hotline 1-888-426-4435 right away.

Alcohol contains ethanol, a seriously toxic chemical compound to dogs which is rapidly absorbed into the dog's system causing central nervous system and respiratory depression. Only small amounts of ethanol can cause toxic effects so it's important to seek medical attention quickly. Inducing vomiting usually will not help. Symptoms include sedation, depression, lethargy, weakness, drunken gait and hypothermia with resulting intoxication, liver failure, coma, seizures and death.

Baking Soda and baking powder in LARGE quantities need to be ingested for toxic effect relative to a dog's size. Typically, these compounds release gases when they react with moisture and heat which can lead to electrolyte abnormalities (low potassium, low calcium and/or high sodium), muscle spasms and /or congestive heart failure.

Bones, cooked, may splinter and puncture or obstruct the digestive tract. Completely ground bones are acceptable. Raw bones are ok but monitor your pet while chewing.

Broccoli in LARGE amounts can cause illness in dogs.

Caffeine (coffee, tea) and **caffeinated items** (such as energy drinks) are similar to the toxic chemical theobromide found in chocolate. Caffeine can damage the heart, lungs, kidney and central nervous system. Symptoms include hyperactivity, excitement, restlessness, and vomiting which can be followed by panting, weakness, rapid heart rate, drunken walking, muscle tremors and convulsions with possible damage to heart, lungs, kidney organs, heart attack, coma or death.

Cat Food is very high in fats and protein and when ingested by a dog, particularly in large amounts or on a regular basis, can lead to potentially deadly pancreatitis.

Chocolate, Coffee and Tea all contain stimulants that cause abnormal heartbeat, seizures and death in dogs. Chocolate is especially dangerous for dogs.

Corn is one of the most frequently genetically modified foods and any form (flour, meal, oil) is not easily digested by dogs which causes the kidneys and liver to work overtime. It is also thought to be the #3 common cause of food allergies in dogs.

Cranberry Juice has a chemical that prevents bacteria from adhering to the wall of the bladder. *Cranberries, however, are safe.*

Dough and Cake Batter The combination of raw bread dough and a dog's body heat can cause the dough to rise inside the stomach resulting in vomiting, severe abdominal pain and bloating. The batter

the canine chef cookbook

used in cakes and pies usually contains raw eggs which could contain salmonella bacteria that may lead to food poisoning.

Fatty Meats can be very dangerous for dogs because they can cause canine pancreatitis, an inflammation of the pancreas. Chronic pancreatitis may develop over time with regular and frequent ingestion of high fat foods or just one fatty meal. Canine pancreatitis is a painful and potentially life-threatening disease. Symptoms can be mild and not that obvious or very painful and severe. Signs include vomiting, diarrhea, no appetite, abdominal pain, dehydration, severe weakness and/or collapse, shock, and fever. Signs of abdominal pain include restlessness, heavy panting, wincing, trembling, arched back, or lying with their front down and their rear end up.

Grapes and Raisins contain an unknown substance that causes kidney failure in dogs.

Greasy, fatty table scraps can cause pancreatitis which is an inflammation of the pancreas caused when too much digestive enzyme is produced. Affected dogs may have bloody vomit or diarrhea and suffer dehydration and even death. This includes dog favorites bacon, ham, and pig ears so feed these sparingly.

Green Unripe Tomatoes, leaves, or stem contain tropane and atropine alkaloids. The tomatine alkaloid present in green unripe fruits and in the tomato plant is highly poisonous to dogs. Excessive drooling, vomiting, diarrhea or constipation are signs of tomato toxicity. Dogs that have ingested green tomatoes will suffer from stomach upsets because tomatine is not efficiently absorbed by the intestines. The cardiac and the central nervous systems of the dog will be directly affected by the toxins present in unripe tomatoes. Ingestion of a considerable amount of unripe tomatoes or leaves and stem of the plant would result in accelerated heartbeats. The toxins will cause tremors, muscle weakness and breathing difficulties which can lead to coma and death.

Hops used in the brewing of beer. Toxicity can occur both before, and after the hops have been used in brewing beer. Dogs particularly like hops soaked in sweet wort. Greyhounds and Labradors are particularly sensitive to hops poisoning. Small amounts of hops can trigger malignant hyperthermia, carbon dioxide levels in blood increase dramatically, high fever, heavy panting, rapid heart-rate resulting in blood toxicity and possible death.

Macadamia Nuts contain an unidentified toxin that causes weakness, tremors, panting and swelling in the legs.

Molds can be toxic to dogs.

Mushrooms contain toxins which are very dangerous for dogs. Symptoms vary dependent on the mushroom and may include nervous system abnormalities, anxiety, restlessness, slow heartbeat, wheezing, urination, salivation, diarrhea, seizure, vomiting possibly resulting in organ failures (including kidneys, liver, and brain), seizure, coma, vomiting, and death. *Common white mushrooms are considered safe for dogs to eat.*

Nutmeg can be toxic or even fatal to dogs. Scientists have not identified the component of nutmeg responsible for the toxic effects. Signs of toxicity include tremors, seizures, central nervous system abnormalities, or death.

Onions, both cooked and raw, contain thiosulphate which can cause digestive upsets, hemolytic anemia, and death.

Pennies dated after 1981 are made from zinc with a thin copper coating. A dog swallowing just one of these pennies can suffer damage to red blood cells and kidney failure due to zinc poisoning.

Pistachio nuts are rich in fat which can contribute to pancreatitis, contains high amounts of phosphorus which can cause bladder stones, and can become contaminated with aflatoxin (produced by a fungus or mold) which can lead to liver failure.

Raw Egg Whites contain avidin which causes vitamin B deficiency, skin problems and skeletal deformities. They can also harbor salmonella or e.coli.

Raw Fish, especially salmon, may contain parasites that are dangerous for dogs.

Raw Yeast/Uncooked Yeast Dough produces ethanol, a type of alcohol. Symptoms can include sedation, depression, lethargy, weakness, drunken gait and hypothermia leading to liver failure, coma, seizures and death.

Rhubarb contains oxalates which trigger abnormalities with the nervous system, kidneys and digestive tract.

Sage contains essential oils and resins that can cause gastrointestinal upset and central nervous system depression to pets.

Salt can produce excessive thirst and urination, or even sodium ion poisoning in pets. Signs that your pet may have eaten too many salty foods include vomiting, diarrhea, depression, tremors, elevated body temperature, seizures and even death. *Sea salt is safe.*

Seeds and Fruit Pits can cause choking or intestinal blockages and some contain cyanide which is toxic to dogs.

Tree nuts, such as walnuts, pecans, pistachios, and Brazil nuts, are often contaminated with very low levels of Aflatoxin which comes from the Aspergillus mold. Although levels are safe for humans, dogs are acutely sensitive to this poison so even low levels of Aflatoxin can be extremely toxic and lead to complications such as gastroenteritis and acute liver failure. They also have a high phosphorus content which causes the formation of bladder stones in dogs. Symptoms of Aflatoxin poisoning include loss of appetite, lethargy, vomiting, orange-colored urine and jaundice, liver failure, blood-tinged vomit and bloody or blackened stools. Symptoms of bladder stones which can result in blockage of the urinary tract include difficulty urinating, frequent "dribbling" urination, bloody urine, and painful urination.

Xylitol causes an insulin reaction in dogs which can lead to liver failure within a few days. It's found in many candies, gums, toothpastes, and pastries.

safe herbs & spices

Seasonings can not only enhance the flavors, they can provide nutrients valuable to a dog's overall wellbeing. Consider growing your own herbs in a raised bed like I do so they are readily available. Fresh is best but dried can also be used. When purchasing always choose organic to avoid any pesticides, herbicides or other containment residues. Fresh herbs can be wrapped in a paper towel and stored in zip lock bags in the refrigerator. Dried herbs should be stored in a dark cool place.

Holistic veterinarians consider these herbs & spices to be safe for healthy dogs with no underlying health issues. Before using any herb or spice consult with your veterinarian for any cautions, possible side effects or conventional drug interactions. Not all herbs and spices are safe for pregnant or lactating dogs or puppies.

Alfalfa is rich in calcium, copper, folate, iron, magnesium, manganese, phosphorous, potassium, silicon and zinc, vitamins A, B1, B12, C, D, E, and K. It is also an antioxidant used to reduce pain and swelling associated with arthritis, nutritive (good for bone building) and diuretic.

Anise seed has anti-oxidant, disease preventing and many health promoting properties. Anise is rich in B complex vitamins, vitamin A and C (anti-oxidants) and important minerals such as copper, iron, magnesium, manganese zinc and potassium.

Basil is rich in essential vitamins, minerals, phyto-nutrients, electrolytes and oils that are essential for optimal health. Basil is an anti-inflammatory, anti-bacterial and anti-oxidant. Basil is well known for its multiple disease preventing and health promoting properties.

Carob is low in fat and sodium, high in fiber, potassium, and calcium, and can improve digestion. It has a natural sweetness and contains very little fat, no caffeine and encourages the absorption of calcium. Even though carob looks like, smells like, and has a taste that is similar to chocolate, it does not contain theobromine, the part of chocolate that is toxic to dogs.

Caraway Seeds are rich in dietary fiber, vital vitamins, and minerals, and anti-oxidants. They are considered a warming herb meaning they help the body stay warm. Caraway seeds are also good for muscle health (anti-contraction), help prevent constipation, and remove a large amount of harmful toxins from the body which helps prevent some cancers.

Catnip isn't just for cats! It contains magnesium, manganese, flavonoids, tannins, vitamins C and E, and essential oils such as neroli, citronellol, nepetalactone, and thymol. It has a mild tranquilizing effect so it's effective for treating restlessness, nervousness, and insomnia. The gas relieving and antispasmodic effect of catnip also makes it excellent for treatment of flatulence, diarrhea, and dyspepsia, and is effective in treating early symptoms of colds, flus, and especially bronchitis. Tip: Put some fresh leaves in drinking water or sprinkle the dried herb (1/8 to ½ teaspoon per pound of food) on a meal.

Cayenne Pepper, a hot and spicy source of vitamin A, vitamin E, vitamin C, vitamin B6, fiber, vitamin K, manganese, and dietary fiber, is the only pepper considered to be safe for dogs. It contains capsaicin which is a potent inhibitor of substance P, a neuropeptide associated with inflammatory processes. Capsaicin is being studied as an effective treatment for sensory nerve fiber disorders, including pain associated with arthritis, psoriasis, and diabetic neuropathy. When animals were fed a diet that contained capsaicin, they had delayed onset of arthritis and also significantly reduced paw inflammation. Cayenne has been shown to reduce blood cholesterol, triglyceride levels, and platelet aggregation while increasing the body's ability to dissolve fibrin, a substance integral to the formation of blood clots. Red peppers are one of the few foods that contain lycopene, a phytochemical that may help prevent various forms of cancer. Cayenne peppers bright red color signals its high content of beta-carotene or pro-vitamin A. These hot peppers may help prevent stomach ulcers by killing ingested bacteria and powerfully stimulating the cells lining the stomach to secrete protective buffering juices that prevent ulcer formation. Finally, they have been found to contain substances that significantly increase thermogenesis (heat production) and oxygen consumption for more than 20 minutes after they are eaten.

Chamomile can be used as a sedative to alleviate anxiety, nervousness, hyperactivity, insomnia, indigestion, gas, and vomiting. Although it's one of the safest herbs, some dogs are allergic to the plant so check for sensitivity. Also limit the use of this herb on pregnant dogs.

Chia Seeds contain large quantities of protein, five times the calcium of milk, boron (a trace mineral that aids in the absorption of calcium into the bones), omega oils 3 and 6, can help regulate blood sugar levels and aid in maintaining a healthy weight. The seeds of chia plants can help maintain healthy cholesterol levels and blood pressure, and reduce risk of heart disease. These seeds have no discernible odor and almost no taste, which means they can be added to your dog's meals without altering the flavors he loves. Seeds can be ground, eaten raw, or added to water, which will cause the seeds to produce what is called chia seed gel. This gel helps clean out intestines and slows digestion, allowing your dog's body to absorb more of the incredible nutrients that chia seeds provide.

Cilantro (Coriander) is considered a digestive aid since it acts mainly on the digestive system moderating the secretion of gastric juices and stimulating the appetite. It relieves gas and indigestion.

Cinnamon has a pungent, slightly sweet flavor. It's recommended to relieve vomiting, aid digestion, and has one of the highest anti-oxidant levels of all food sources. It can help remove the aflatoxins present in foods and is recommended for keeping teeth clean and fighting bad breath. Cassis cinnamon is what you will find in most grocery stores. It contains high levels of coumarin (5 %) which is a naturally occurring toxin with the potential to damage the liver in high doses and found to be carcinogenic in rodents. I use Ceylon cinnamon from the health store which is sweeter and contains either undetectable levels or traces (0.4 %) of coumarin.

Dandelion contains vitamins A, C, D, E, K, B complex, potassium, calcium, iron, thiamin, choline, lecithin, and riboflavin. This herb is also a strong but safe diuretic and liver stimulant, and its rich supply of potassium replenishes the precious mineral lost in the urine. The root has the ability to stimulate bile production by more than 50 percent, and increases bile flow to the gallbladder which proves to be helpful for dogs suffering from liver congestion, gallstones, and other forms of liver problems. The flowers are high in lecithin and have useful pain reducing qualities making it useful as a mild painkiller. Tip: The flowers and greens can be dried and then sprinkled on the dog's food as a supplement. Alternatively, make a leaf tea by boiling the greens in unsalted vegetable or meat broth. (Daily intake: One teaspoon of dried herb for each 20 pounds of body weight.)

Dill improves appetite, digestion and flatulence. It eases bloating due to gas and improves the digestive process because the gut gets better at extracting nutrients from foods and fewer nutrients are lost in excrement. It's considered an antispasmodic which can help relax the colon and relieve constipation and helps to stop diarrhea and dysentery. Its antimicrobial action helps freshen the mouth when chewed or washed with an extract of dill. It's known to activate an enzyme called glutathione S-transferase which neutralizes carcinogens and generally detoxifies the body and has an antihistamine effect that helps clear respiratory congestion caused by allergies or cough.

Fennel contains protein, vitamin A, vitamin C, niacin, calcium, iron, magnesium, phosphorous, potassium, zinc, copper, and omega-6 fatty acids. It acts as a detoxifier and strong digestive aid.

Fennel Seeds are used mainly as a digestive and have been known to normalize the appetite, aid weight loss, treat flatulence, calm the digestive tract, cleanse the liver, help with detoxifying the body as a whole, and is a natural diuretic.

Flax Seed, also known as linseeds, plays a significant role in canine cardiovascular health and skin and coat health since it is an important source of fiber and antioxidants, and it may have anti-tumor properties as well.

Garlic contains germanium, an anti-cancer agent, helps to regulate blood pressure, helps strengthen the body's defenses against allergies, and regulate blood sugar levels. It's considered an aid to fighting and treating diabetes and liver, heart and kidney disease. It provides vitamin A, B, B2, C, calcium, potassium, and zinc. It's a natural flea repellent and de-wormer.

Ginger is an antioxidant and anti-inflammatory used to treat digestive upset, nausea, gas, motion sickness, heart problems, joint inflammation due to arthritic conditions, reduce fever, and is also effective as an anti-infective against viruses. It can decrease blood sugar levels, and increase absorption of all oral medications. *Too much ginger may cause nausea, especially when given on an empty stomach, and can affect how well blood clots. Do not give to a dog with a gastric ulcer or pregnant dogs.*

Green Tea is rich in anti-oxidants, has a calming effect, and many studies have shown that the polyphenols such as EGCG may enhance the human body's ability to prevent cancer. It does have the ability to cause cancer cell suicide (apoptosis). There are no studies showing the effect of EGCG in dogs with cancer. However, most agree it is unlikely to cause harm and may help. The maximum dose you should feed your dog is 500mg on a full stomach. *Make sure you use de-caffeinated and know it can interfere with some chemotherapy drugs if your dog is undergoing cancer treatment.*

Kelp (seaweed) is a nutritional powerhouse containing vitamin A, vitamin C, vitamin E, vitamin K, folate, iodine, calcium, iron, magnesium, phosphorous, potassium, zinc, copper, manganese and selenium. Kelp benefits thyroid function, promotes heart health, helps fight and prevent cancer, is a powerful anti-oxidant, aids in healing skin disorders and enhancing coat health.

Licorice is an effective anti-inflammatory due to the presence of glycyrrhizin which has a similar chemical structure to that of natural corticosteroids released by the adrenal glands. Glycyrrhizin stimulates the adrenals and is useful for treating Addison's disease. The herb also acts on the digestive system by promoting cell growth and alleviating ulcers and is also beneficial in treating liver toxicity. For the upper respiratory tracts, licorice root has long been used to alleviate coughs and ease discomfort brought on by bronchitis due to its demulcent, anti-flammatory, and expectorant properties. *Licorice can raise sugar levels in blood and should be used with caution in diabetic dogs. Do not give licorice to dogs with heart disease.*

Milk Thistle is well known as a "liver herb" both for humans and pets. It contains a flavonoid compound called silymarin which is a combination of several other active compounds. Extensive studies around the world have found that silymarin is safe and effective in treating a variety of liver diseases and other conditions, from kidney disease to mushroom or lead poisoning. It works by displacing toxins trying to bind to the liver causing it to regenerate more quickly. In addition, silymarin can work as an antioxidant for the liver by scavenging free radicals and stabilizing liver cell membranes. It also stimulates the production of new liver cells.

Holistic veterinarians (and some conventional ones as well) have long been using milk thistle to treat dog liver disease. It has an excellent safety record and no known adverse drug interactions, although taking too much of the herb at a time can sometimes cause an upset stomach, gas, or mild diarrhea.

Oregano is a rich natural source of fiber and omega-3 fatty acids. It contains vitamin K, anti-oxidants, iron, manganese, fiber, and is a natural source of omega-3 fatty acids. It is renowned for its anti-bacterial, anti-viral, anti-fungal and anti-parasitic properties.

Parsley Leaves are packed with B vitamins, C vitamins, carotene, iron and calcium. In addition to its use for bad breath, it can stimulate the kidneys to filter out toxins and increase urine.

Peppermint is known for its soothing effect of an upset stomach, respiratory infections, viral infections and skin conditions. It provides effective relief of flatulence and indigestion. Its anti-parasitic medical properties are an alternate solution in the treatment of worms for dogs. It is an antispasmodic, stimulates circulation, good for arthritis, dysplasia, sprains and strains, and works well with ginger to treat motion sickness. *Because one of the key constituents of peppermint is menthol, the oil should be kept away from your pets' eyes and sensitive skin areas. It can be used topically or orally.*

Rosemary is high in fiber, rich in vitamins, anti-oxidant, anti-inflammatory, anti-allergic, anti-fungal, anti-septic, disease preventing and health promoting properties. *Rosemary is known to cause seizures in some dogs*

Sea Salt, in small amounts, is considered safe for dogs. It provides sodium, which is necessary for life. It helps with muscle contraction and expansion, nerve stimulation, the proper functioning of the adrenals, chloride which helps produce acids necessary to digest protein and enzymes for carbohydrate digestion necessary for proper brain functioning and growth, and finally, magnesium which is important for producing enzymes, nerve transmission, bone formation, forming tooth enamel, and resistance to heart disease.

Spirulina is a microscopic algae in the shape of a perfect spiral coil. It contains the most concentration of nutrients known in any food, plant, grain or herb. It's the highest protein food (over 60% all digestible vegetable protein with the highest concentration of beta carotene), vitamin B-12, iron and trace minerals, and the rare essential fatty acid GLA (gamma-linoleic acid). Both test tube studies and animal based research suggest that spirulina may help to strengthen the immune system, improve gastrointestinal health, aid in detoxification, reduce the rate of cancer, and help allergies.

Thyme contains vitamin K, iron, manganese, calcium, fiber, tryptophan, phytochemicals and anti-oxidants. It has antiseptic, anti-spasmodic, anti-bacterial properties, and is thought to have anti-cancer properties. It's good for the skin, respiratory system, brain function and gastrointestinal health.

Turmeric has a peppery, warm and bitter flavor and a mild fragrance slightly reminiscent of orange and ginger. It is best known as one of the ingredients used to make curry but it also gives mustard its bright yellow color. Curcumin, the principle active component in turmeric, is a potent anti-inflammatory and antibacterial agent that shows promise in the prevention and treatment of cancer among other conditions. It is generally found to be safe for dogs with veterinarians frequently recommending the addition of turmeric (up to a quarter of a teaspoon per day for every 10 pounds of weight) to a dog's diet if they have been diagnosed with cancer. Turmeric can also be good for reducing arthritis inflammation and pain in pets. You can use powder, crushed or fresh root.

HERBS & SPICES WHICH ARE NOT SAFE FOR DOGS:

Cocoa
Comfrey
Paprika
Pennyroyal
Pepper
Table Salt
Tea Tree Oil
Nutmeg
Mace
Ma Haung (Ephedra)
Wormwood

Making Oat Flour

safe flours

Just like we enjoy different breads and crackers, dogs also enjoy the different flavors and textures. This is a basic guideline to replacing flours in a recipe with a different flour due to allergies or flavor preferences.

Whole Wheat Flour
A strong nutty flavored flour with a firm texture and rich brown color. It keeps 1 to 2 months in the refrigerator and up to 6 months in the freezer.

White Whole Wheat Flour
A milder tasting flour with a lighter texture than whole wheat flour. It keeps 1 to 2 months in the refrigerator and up to 6 months in the freezer.

Oat flour
A gluten free flour with a slightly sweet nutty flavor providing a wonderful lightness and moisture. It keeps 3 months in a dark cabinet or 6 months in the freezer. (1 1/3 cup = 1 cup whole wheat flour)

Barley Flour
A moist, sweet, nutlike flavor with a low gluten content. It has a short shelf life but will keep up to 4 months in the freezer. (1 1/3 cup = 1 cup whole wheat flour)

Millet Flour
A sweet tasting gluten free flour that imparts a lighter texture with a crunchy crust but can be too dry and crumbly. It keeps up to 2 months in the refrigerator and up to 6 months in the freezer. (1 cup = 1 cup whole wheat flour)

Brown Rice flour
A gluten free flour with a strong, nutty flavor. Because it can go rancid quickly, keep it stored 4 to 5 months in the refrigerator or up to 1 year in the freezer. (7/8 cup = 1 cup whole wheat flour)

Rye flour
A low gluten flour with a strong earthy taste. It produces a sticky dough so you may want to wet your hands with water or lightly oil them. It keeps for 2 months in the refrigerator or 6 months in the freezer. (1¼ cup = 1 cup whole wheat flour)

Spelt Flour
A low gluten flour from a cereal grain in the wheat family. It has a nutty and slightly sweet flavor similar to wheat flour. Be careful not to over mix it or risk having a crumbly texture. It keeps for 2 months in a dark cabinet or 6 months in the freezer. (1 cup = 1 cup whole wheat flour)

Grain Free Flours

Chickpea Flour (also called garbanzo flour)
A gluten free, grain free flour which absorbs liquids without clumping and adds a mellow, buttery taste. It keeps 2 to 3 months in the refrigerator and up to 6 months in the freezer. (3/4 cup = 1 cup whole wheat flour)

Coconut Flour
A gluten free, grain free flour with a sweetness because of the natural sugars in the coconut. This dry flour soaks up liquids so you will need to increase the liquids in the recipe you are using. It also doesn't stick together well so be sure to add eggs which allow it to bond and form batter. It keeps up to 1 year in a dark cabinet. (1/3 cup + 1 egg = 1 cup whole wheat flour)

Potato Flour
A grain free flour with a soft, moist texture which makes dough easier to shape and handle. Because the starch attracts and holds water, you need to add potato flour to the other dry ingredients first and whisk together before adding to liquids to avoid clumping. Potato flour is the entire potato dried and ground whereas potato starch is only the starch. It keeps up to 6 months in the freezer. (5/8 cup = 1 cup whole wheat flour)

Quinoa Flour
A gluten free, grain free flour with a very mild hint of nuttiness that needs to be mixed with other flours to avoid a gluey texture. It can go rancid easily so store in the refrigerator or freezer. (1 cup = 1 cup whole wheat flour)

Tapioca Flour
A starchy, grain free flour with a slightly sweet flavor that improves the texture of baked goods and helps add crispness to crusts and chew to baked goods. It's an extremely smooth flour which makes for a great thickener in sauces and soups since it never discolors and contains no discernible taste or smell. It can also be used to replace corn starch which is detrimental to dogs. It keeps up to 3 years in a dark cabinet. (1 cup = 1 cup whole wheat flour)

Buckwheat Flour
A gluten free, grain free flour which is actually a fruit seed related to rhubarb and sorrel. It has a strong nutty taste that can overpower the other flavors in a recipe so it's usually mixed with other types of flour, such as rice or oat, to produce better results. (7/8 cup = 1 cup whole wheat flour)

the incredible egg

One egg has only 75 calories but 7 grams of high-quality protein, 5 grams of fat, and 1.6 grams of saturated fat, along with iron, phosphorous, selenium and vitamins A, B12, B2 and B5, minerals, and carotenoids. Eggs help build muscle, strengthen the hair, and repair tissue and it's a powerhouse of disease-fighting nutrients like lutein and zeaxanthin.

Raw eggs are not generally recommended due to the presence of the naturally occurring protein avidin in raw egg whites. Occasional consumption is not an issue, but excess avidin interferes with the functioning of biotin in the body. Biotin, more commonly known as vitamin H or B7, is essential for the growth of cells, metabolism of fat, and transference of carbon dioxide.

The Fresh Test

Egg shells are porous so over time the liquid in the egg evaporates and is replaced by outside air resulting in more buoyant eggs. Test your eggs by filling a bowl with cold water and placing the egg in it. If it sinks to the bottom, it's fresh. If it sinks to the bottom but stands on its point, it's still good but needs to be used soon. If it floats to the top, toss it.

Boiling Eggs

1. Place eggs in a pot and cover with an inch of water.
2. Bring the water to a boil over high heat.
3. Remove from heat, cover, and let rest for 15 to 17 minutes.
4. Pour out the hot water and fill with enough cold water to cover the eggs.
5. Let cool and then remove the shells.

Boiled eggs can be kept in the refrigerator for about 7 days.

Scrambling Eggs

The key to making perfect scrambled eggs is whisking the eggs thoroughly and vigorously before cooking them which incorporates air and volume to produce fluffier scrambled eggs. Scramble the eggs on low heat in a sauce pan constantly working them with a silicone spatula to reduce the risk of browning and overcooking. They will continue to cook with residual heat which can dry them out so take them off the heat when they still look wet but not runny. Season the eggs at the end of cooking since the salt can break down the eggs making them watery.

Removing the Egg Shells

Once the eggs are boiled it's time to place them in a bowl of cold water to let them set. An easy way to remove the shell is to gently crack the egg and then re-submerge it into the cold water for about an hour. This will allow the water to get in between the shell and the egg making it easier to peel.

Grinding Egg Shells for Calcium

1. Wash the empty egg shells in warm water until all of the egg white is removed being careful not to remove the papery thin membrane attached to the inside of the shell since it contains important nutrients for your pet's joints which helps with arthritis.
2. Lay the broken shells out on paper towels and allow them to air dry thoroughly. I then store them in an extra egg carton in the cabinet until I have enough to grind.
3. When ready to grind first bake the egg shells at 300 degrees for ten minutes to remove the mineral oil coating used to keep the eggs fresh. This step is only necessary for store bought eggs not farm fresh eggs.
4. Break the egg shells up into small pieces and grind them into a fine powder in a coffee grinder you have NOT ground coffee in. I have a grinder specifically for Kirby so I don't have to worry about what might have been left behind that can harm him. You can put the egg shells in a plastic bag and use a rolling pin to grind them.
5. Store in a glass jar with a tight fitting lid in a dry place like a kitchen cabinet for up to two months.

Add ¼ teaspoon per pound of meat in a recipe or ¼ teaspoon per cup of prepared food.
1 medium sized egg shell equals 1 teaspoon of powder.

make it egg free

Kirby enjoys scrambled eggs and tuna, plain boiled eggs, and eggs in a lot of his treats and meals. I even save the eggshells to grind up for the calcium they provide.

However, there are many dogs with allergies who must avoid eggs. If that's your dog, you can change any recipe with eggs as an ingredient into an egg free recipe. Just choose one of the replacement ingredients below that has the flavor to best compliment the other ingredients for each egg.

¼ cup unsweetened applesauce
¼ cup mashed banana
¼ cup plain Greek yogurt
3 tablespoons pureed fruit
2 tablespoons potato starch
1 tablespoon ground flax seed in ¼ cup very hot water. Let sit 10 minutes.

garlic is good

As I've been sharing my recipes one of the comments that keeps coming up is "garlic will kill a dog!" I strongly beg to differ and Kirby, at a healthy active six years of age, can back me up. However, I'm not basing my decision to use garlic in my recipes based on flavor and aroma (which is delicious) but on reputable holistic veterinarians who have been using garlic for years and the research efforts of experts who are proving that garlic is actually good for dogs.

Both garlic and onion contain thiosulphate, the substance responsible for causing Heinz Factor anemia in dogs and cats. Garlic DOES NOT CONTAIN THE SAME CONCENTRATION of this compound! In fact, it is barely traceable and readily excreted (not stored in the body).

The Benefits

The reason garlic is added to dog food and treats is because it has many health benefits. It's a powerful, natural broad-spectrum antibiotic, an antioxidant, anti-allergen, antibacterial, anti-fungal, anti-protozoan, anti-viral and anti-carcinogen.

Garlic is high in calcium, potassium, zinc, vitamin A, B, B2, and C. It helps and/or treats asthma, environmental allergies, diabetes, diarrhea, fatigue, and the maintenance of healthy liver function. It's been proven to help dogs with suppressed immune systems and those fighting cancer by giving a boost to bloodstream cells that kill bad microbes and cancer cells. It helps prevent a variety of cancers such as bladder cancer, colon cancer, prostate cancer, lung cancer, rectal cancer, and stomach cancer and is used to treat some forms of cancer such as bladder and prostate cancer. It's known to have detoxifying effects which can help the liver get rid of toxins from the body. It can help older and overweight dogs because it can prevent blood clots and reduce cholesterol levels and fat build up in the arteries. Many believe it helps ward off fleas.

Safe Dosages

Too much of anything is bad for you. Even vitamins and minerals can be detrimental in large daily amounts. Did you know it's been proven that too much water can kill you? The same goes with garlic and dogs. At some level, everything has the potential to be toxic.

- Dr. Martin Goldstein (author of The Nature of Animal Healing) recommends adding garlic to homemade pet food and feeds garlic to his own cats and dogs on a regular basis.
- Dr. Messonnier (author of The Natural Vet's Guide to Preventing and Treating Cancer in Dogs) recommends one clove of fresh garlic per 10 to 30 pounds of weight a day to boost the immune system and cancer prevention.
- Dr. Pitcairn (author of The Complete Guide to Natural Health for Dogs and Cats) recommends the following amount of fresh garlic for dogs, according to their size:

10 to 15 pounds - half a clove
20 to 40 pounds - 1 clove
45 to 70 pounds - 2 cloves
75 to 90 pounds - 2 and a half cloves
100 pounds and over - 3 cloves

The Whole Dog Journal recommends garlic as a good addition to any raw diet. Their advice is that you can safely feed 1 clove of garlic for every 20 lbs. of body weight.

As with most herbs, at least one to two days off per week or a periodic week off from garlic is a good idea.

Warnings

When used in the dosage provided above, garlic is safe for pregnant dogs. The only caution for pregnant dogs is that if ingested in large quantities it can flavor the milk of lactating females. Don't give garlic to puppies that are 6 months of age or younger.

Garlic is high in insoluble fiber and sulfur compounds so as a general rule it is best not to give fresh garlic to dogs that have IBS or colitis.

Check with your veterinarian if your dog is on any medications. Garlic may increase the rate at which cyclosprine is broken down by the body so it might decrease its effectiveness, and can slow down blood clotting which would affect the efficacy of a blood thinner.

Some garlic from China has been found to be contaminated with high levels of arsenic, lead and added sulfites.

Tip

To get rid of the smell on your hands, rinse them under water while rubbing them with a stainless steel bar or spoon.

If I still haven't convinced you of the benefits and safety of garlic, then just omit it from any recipe.

safe food colors

Kirby doesn't care if his treats are decorated but sometimes I just want to be a little more creative. I consider commercial food coloring to be unsafe for dogs since the synthetic or unnatural ingredients used in food coloring is considered unsafe for both children and adults. These artificial food dyes have been linked directly to multiple forms of cancer in adults in addition to behavior problems and hyperactivity disorder in children.

You can purchase safe, all natural food dyes like India Tree Natural Decorating Colors but it's quite expensive. Even better you can make your own safe colors. Each ingredient will impart its own flavor which can become too strong if you are trying to create a vivid color. Another important factor is the amount of juice needed to achieve a deeper color which will end up making the "frosting" too runny. I prefer the powder forms which are so simple to make and can be stored for up to a year.

Safe Food Color Options

> YELLOW - turmeric powder
> ORANGE - carrots or pumpkin (Juice or pulverize).
> RED/PINK - beets or raspberries (Use the juice from canned beets or pulverize a raw beet. Adds little flavor.)(Crush or pulverize the raspberries.)
> PURPLE - red cabbage (Boil the cabbage.)
> GREEN - spinach, spirulina. (Boil the leaves. Adds no flavor.)
> BLUE - blueberries or blackberries (Crush or pulverize the berries.)

The Basic Recipe

1. Bring 2 cups of water to a boil and then add the sliced fruit or vegetable.
2. Let simmer for several hours.
3. Use immediately.

The Powder Recipe

1. Lay out thinly sliced vegetables or fruit leaving room for the air to circulate all around.
2. Dehydrate or bake at lowest setting for 2 to 6 hours until completely dried.
3. Grind into a fine powder and store in an air tight container for up to a year.

It will only take a pinch or two to color your icing.

soak those grains

Even though dogs are believed to be descended from wolves, they are not genetically the same. This genetic transformation is thought to have occurred over tens of thousands of years ago leading to numerous genetic variations, or mutations, between wolves and dogs. So far 10 key genes have been identified that demonstrate the domesticated dogs' increased ability to digest starch and fat. It is speculated that these mutations allowed the early ancestors of the modern dog to thrive on the discarded wheat and other crop products of farmers which led to their domestication.

A dog's short digestive tract is much less specialized for digesting grains in their raw form. However, they are opportunistic feeders that can digest and utilize the starch from grains that have been converted by the cooking process. Simply put, they can't digest grains unless they are "predigested". Once converted, the nutrients are fully available for absorption.

Kirby enjoys a variety of grains in his meals so I have learned soaking makes them easier to digest and releases the needed enzymes to be more nutritionally available. (I don't soak the grain if I am grinding it to use as flour in a treat recipe).

Grains contain phytic acid which is present largely in the bran. This binds to minerals, such as calcium, magnesium, iron, copper and zinc, making them unavailable for absorption in the intestine. A diet high in improperly prepared whole grains may lead to digestive problems, allergies, serious mineral deficiencies and bone loss.

Soaking them in water activates germination which is thought to reduce the enzyme inhibitors. For example, soaking activates the enzyme phytase which then neutralizes phytic acid. Through the soaking process, the enzyme inhibitors are 'neutralized,' other beneficial enzymes are activated and the vitamin content increases, especially the B vitamins, vitamin C and carotene.

What this means is that normal digestion depends on enzymes working to break down the food starting with the saliva and running the course through the entire digestive system. Enzyme inhibitors found in whole grains interfere with this normal digestion by stopping the enzymes from doing their jobs properly and stress out the pancreas.

It's been found that the difference between soaked grains and unsoaked grains has a profound impact on the digestive system. Also since soaking can break down gluten, those with sensitivities are better able to tolerate soaked grains.

the canine chef cookbook

These are the standard guidelines for most grains:
> Oats, rye, barley, and wheat should always be soaked.
> Buckwheat, rice, spelt and millet can be soaked less frequently.
> Whole rice and whole millet contain even less phytates so it's not necessary to always soak.
> Flax seed does not require soaking if eaten in small amounts.

Directions

1. Measure out 1 cup of grain and pour into a glass jar or other container with a lid.
2. Add 2 tablespoons of an acid.*
3. Add 2 cups of water. Stir and let it soak for 8-12 hours or overnight at room temperature. It's not necessary to refrigerate the grain while it's soaking.
4. Drain the grain in a large colander and rinse, rinse, rinse with cool water. The grain is now ready to be cooked. Soaked grains can be stored in a covered container in the refrigerator for one to two days.

* Any soaking method will increase the nutritional qualities of a grain, but for optimal nutritional value, choose an acid such as plain yogurt, kefir, buttermilk, vinegar, or lemon juice. Cultured products provide beneficial bacteria like lactobacilli which can begin to pre-digest the grain. The vinegar and lemon juice offer an alternative acid for those with true milk allergies. All acid choices discourage spoilage from unfriendly bacteria during a long soak.

homemade meals

Kirby's meals consist of 90 percent homemade foods and 10 percent quality commercial foods. He gets less than a small handful of crunchy kibble in the morning in one of his interactive toys. About once a month I'll scramble up some eggs and tuna or sardines for a special breakfast. He eats roughly one cup homemade food in the evening, less if he's had treats during the day. He receives a hip and joint treat every morning and a pet multi-vitamin every evening. He also gets one treat at bedtime. He adores bully sticks so he gets three to four each month. I do a lot of research so I know he is eating a healthy diet, and just to be safe, he sees his veterinarian every few months.

He is now six years old with a sparkle in his eyes and the energy of a puppy. His easy to manage coat is soft and shiny. He has no skin problems or allergies of any type. He doesn't have bad breath and his teeth are still white. I do brush them two to three times a week using a finger brush with a dog toothpaste. He rarely becomes ill, and when he has, we were able to find the source: a recalled treat, a recalled kibble, a shared can of Vienna sausages, some chocolate he got into, and a nasty dog bite when he was a year old. His weight maintains around 15 pounds which seems like a lot until you realize he is all muscle from the Dachshund. His veterinarian always says he can stand to lose a pound or two but as long as she can easily feel his ribs he's fine.

I prepare large batches which I then freeze in individual serving size portions. Some will say you must measure this and add that to achieve a balanced meal. The guidelines I follow are much simpler.

Variety

A homemade diet should include a variety of meats (beef, lamb, deer, chicken, turkey, fish), vegetables (green, yellow, orange), and grains. I like to use various dog safe herbs and spices because, one, he enjoys the flavors, and two, there are many health benefits. I was surprised to discover how much he likes cayenne pepper! I also mix in organ meats, cooked eggs, low fat cottage cheese, yogurt, kefir, and applesauce throughout the month. For the most part I avoid pork and duck since they are fatty meats which can attribute to pancreatis.

I also keep his consumption of commercial kibble to a minimum amount. He loves the crunch but commercial kibble is extruded, meaning the moisture has been removed. A dog needs at least 70 percent moisture in their diet so digesting dry kibble requires the body to provide sufficient moisture to reconstitute the food in the digestive tract. This becomes stressful to multiple organ systems but most notably the kidneys.

Dogs are descendants from wolves which eat an almost entirely meat diet hence they are carnivores. Yes, dogs can survive as vegans but I do not believe they would thrive at their ultimate best. Wolves will kill an animal and eat everything but the large bones. This includes the stomach of small animals that have eaten vegetation and grains so they become a part of the wolf's diet. Since the vegetables and grains have been digested, I finely chop the vegetables and pre-soak the grains to break them down for Kirby's body to absorb the nutrients.

Another controversy I've come across is that dogs do not require carbohydrates as they don't supply as much nutrition to dogs as animal products do and are difficult for dogs to digest. Researchers are now finding that dogs have evolved to eat a more varied diet than their wolf ancestors.

I personally think Kirby needs carbs to maintain his high energy. I do help along the digestion aspect by soaking the grains for several hours to break them down and then rinsing to remove a lot of the starch before cooking or adding them in his meals. I also cook them to the point of mush rather than el dente.

Many think when their dog has a skin allergy it's due to grains, but more often it's usually a protein. Eating the same protein day in and day out can cause a dog to become allergic to that very protein. I'm leaning toward the reason Kirby has not developed any allergies is because he eats a rotational diet. By feeding a wide variety of different foods, I feel we are achieving an overall complete and balanced diet.

Calcium

An important element when feeding homemade meals is that you must supplement calcium especially if your dog is not receiving raw bones on a regular basis.

Adult dogs need around 800 to 1,000 mg of calcium per pound of food fed. They also require the calcium to be supplied in a proper proportion to phosphorus. The ideal calcium:phosphorus ratio in the canine diet is between 1:1 and 2:1. Meat contains a lot of phosphorus, so the more meat a diet contains, the more calcium will be required to reach the correct calcium:phosphorus ratio. Adding 800 to 1,000 mg of calcium will provide the correct calcium:phosphorus ratio even for a high meat diet.

My solution is ground eggshells. One eggshell provides one teaspoon of ground egg shell which contains 2,000 mg of calcium. I don't want to give him too much since many fresh foods provide calcium, so I add ¼ teaspoon ground eggshell (500 mg) per each pound of meat used in a recipe.

Multi-Vitamins

Just like humans, I find that a complete multi-vitamin and mineral supplement made for dogs is needed to round out the daily nutritional requirements. I don't have the time or knowledge to measure and account for every vitamin and mineral Kirby needs every day. Giving him a daily multi-vitamin takes care of that for me.

I eat healthy foods and fed my children a variety of healthy meals along with a daily vitamin. I treat Kirby the same way.

I am not a veterinarian or nutrition expert so I am not advising anyone on how they should feed their dog. I am a pet parent who, through extensive research and practice, is raising a healthy, vibrant animal in the best way I know how. I simply believe that when good food goes in, healthy benefits shine out.

portion control

I do bake and cook a lot for Kirby but he doesn't eat as much as you would think. If I let him free feed he would be one fat boy considering how much he loves food. I like to know how much he is eating, and if he isn't eating, which is a sign something is wrong, so I believe in portion control. The meals I cook for him are frozen in individual sizes for future feedings while the treats are shared with other dogs.

Are you wondering how much to feed your dog each day? It's recommended that a dog should eat 2-3 percent of his total body weight daily. Puppies would need a bit more while older or inactive dogs would need less. There are two ways to figure this.

The first is the easiest and the one I've always used. Multiply your dog's weight by 16 to get his total body weight in ounces. For example, Kirby weighs 15 pounds so 15 lb. x 16 oz. = 240 oz. which is his total body weight in ounces. Next divide that number by 2 percent for the total minimum amount of daily food to feed (240 oz. x .02 = 4.8 oz.) and divide by 3 percent for the total maximum amount of daily food to feed (240 oz. x .03 = 7.2 oz.) One cup is 8 oz. so we stay pretty close.

The other way is to count calories. I don't count my calories consumed so I'm not going to count his. Having said this, I have a friend who counts every calorie she consumes so this is a personal choice as to what works best for you. One thing I do want to mention is I don't eat a lot of sugar and fat so neither does Kirby.

Dogs weighing less than 20 pounds require 40 calories per pound per day. For instance, Kirby weighs 15 pounds so he needs 600 calories per day (15 lb. x 40 = 600). Dogs that weigh over 100 pounds usually need about 15 calories per pound of body weight per day. For example, a 100 pound German Shepard will need roughly 1,500 calories per day (100 lb. x 15 = 1,500).

You can feed one daily meal or divide it into two feedings. I used to feed Kirby one meal in the evening but he seemed to be starving by meal time so I changed to two daily meals which suits him better - a small amount of kibble in the morning and a nourishing meal in the evening. These are standard guidelines which can be adjusted to fit your dog. Is he too thin? Add more. Is he overactive? Add more. Is he on the chubby side? Add less. Is he laid back or a senior? Add less.

For an accurate calorie count, I use the recipe analysis at http://www.caloriecount.com for the recipes.

the recipes

baked treats

Bake a batch of love for your pups. Try something sweet or savory, meaty or meatless, crunchy or soft. You'll soon discover what your pup loves best.

Baked Rice Cakes 53
Banana Carob Pupcakes 54
Bananaramas 55
Barkin Bacon Bites 56
Blueberry Pupcakes 57
B'oat Bites 58
Butternut Bliss Biscuits 60
Cajun Bacun Biscuits 61
Carrot Pupcakes 63
Cheeseburgers 65
Cheese Nips Kinda 67
Chicken Cordon Bleu 69
Coconut Catters 70
Ezy Cheezy 71
Grrreat Granola Bars 72
Green Eggs & Ham 75
Harvest Pumpkin Balls 77
Lamb Nuggets 78
Liver Lover's Meaty Bones 79
Liver Pate' Bites 81
Milk Bones 83
Mississippi Mud Puppies 84
Pawsome Pumpkin Pupcakes 85
Peanut Butter Paws 86
Pesto Puppers 87
Pumpkin Cran Muffins 91
Puppermint Patties 92
Pupperoni Pizza Pies 93
Sweet Potato Puffs 94
Tasty Tuna Treats 95
The Elvis Biscuit 96
The Great Plumpkin 97
The Kirbylicious Barkday Cake 98
Turkey N Rye Meaty Bones 99

little morsels

Not all ovens are the same so adjust the baking times to your specific oven.

To make the treats really crispy turn off the oven after baking and leave the treats in the oven for a few hours or overnight.

I sometimes use an egg wash to make the hard treats shiny. Whisk an egg white in a small cup and brush over tops with a silicone brush before baking.

I use Ceylon cinnamon which imparts a lighter taste. If you are using Cassia cinnamon which is what is sold in most grocery stores, reduce the amount listed in a recipe by half.

Always use pure pumpkin not pumpkin pie filling which is loaded with ingredients your dog should not eat.

Always use pure maple syrup not pancake syrup which is loaded with ingredients your dog should not eat.

I use fresh herbs from my garden whenever possible but I understand many may not have that luxury. For convenience I have listed the dry/ground herb ingredient amounts in the recipes with a conversion chart for using fresh herbs under The Pantry.

Want to make super quick treats? Pour the batter from any of my pupcake recipes, or any loose batter, into a baker's bag. Using a wide tip, squeeze small dabs onto a lined baking sheet. Bake at 350 degrees until golden brown on bottom.

Unless otherwise noted, these treats will keep in an airtight container for a week, in the refrigerator for up to two weeks, or up to 4 months in the freezer. Always watch for mold when storing soft treats.

baked rice cakes

This recipe should be called "saving a mistake". I was attempting to dogify Japanese rice balls called onigiri which are shaped into rounds or triangles by hand with a filling in the center. They are then wrapped in plastic wrap or Nori, strips of seaweed, and kept in the refrigerator for quick lunches or snacks.

Trust me when they say sticky rice, they mean sticky rice! I tried to form the balls which should have stuck together so I could push the fish filling into the rice. This is where it all failed. I even tried smooshing the mixture into little silicon molds to no avail. Dogs have difficulty digesting the starches in rice which is why I use parboiled rice or soak my rice first. Hence, no onigiri for Kirby.

I had to improvise to try to save the ingredients so I dumped everything back into the bowl. I knew adding a couple of eggs would work as a binder which indeed saved my cakes. I suppose these would be a cross between an onigiri and an arancini, an Italian rice ball. A match made in heaven?

Ingredients

1 cup parboiled rice
¼ teaspoon sea salt
2 strips kombu kelp
1 (4.25 oz.) can mackerel fillets
1 (3.75 oz.) can herring fillets
2 large eggs

Directions

1. Cook the rice according to the package directions.
2. In a small bowl mash the mackerel and herring. You can use canned tuna if preferred.
3. When rice is done, mix in the finely chopped kelp. It can be dried or you can cook it by placing the strips in a pot of water, bringing to a boil and then simmering for 20 minutes.
4. Add the beaten eggs and mix thoroughly. I find this easiest to do with my hands.
5. Tightly press the mixture evenly into oil sprayed mini muffin tins.
6. Refrigerate for at least 30 minutes.
7. Bake at 350 degrees for 20-25 minutes until the tops are crispy and browned.

Prep Time: 40 minutes	Cook Time: 25 minutes	
Yields: 36 mini muffins	Calories: 38 each	Calories from fat: 11 each

banana carob pupcakes

These tasty little bites of goodness will satisfy your dog's sweet tooth without being overly sweet. Kirby prefers savory over sweet so I usually make these in mini muffin tins. I really couldn't tell if he had a preference for frosted or plain and none of the other dogs seem too picky. They're perfect by themselves or frost them up for a special occasion. Either way the pups will be happy you baked!

Ingredients

3 mashed medium bananas
¼ cup plain Greek yogurt
½ cup unsweetened applesauce
1 large egg
3 tablespoons coconut oil
2 teaspoons pure vanilla extract
1 ½ cups whole wheat flour
1 ½ teaspoons baking soda
¾ teaspoon ground cinnamon
¼ teaspoon sea salt
½ cup carob chips

Directions

1. In a bowl stir together the wet ingredients.
2. In another bowl combine the dry ingredients and add to the wet ingredients stirring just until combined.
3. Fold in the carob chips.
4. Divide the batter evenly in oil sprayed muffin tins.
5. Bake at 350 degrees for 15 minutes or until done using a toothpick inserted in the center to test.
6. Remove from the oven and let cool for 5 minutes before gently removing and placing on a cooling rack until completely cool.

Store individually wrapped in saran wrap in the refrigerator for up to a week. When ready to serve top with some frosting.

Prep Time: 15 minutes	Cook Time: 15 minutes	
Yields: 36 mini muffins	Calories: 59 each	Calories from fat: 21 each

bananaramas

Just enough sweetness to satisfy that sweet tooth and a whole lotta goodness! Bananas are very low in saturated fat, cholesterol and sodium, a good source of dietary fiber, vitamin C, potassium and manganese, and a very good source of vitamin B6.

Ingredients

1 ½ cups oat flour
2 cups brown rice flour
1 large egg
¼ cup ground flax seed
½ cup dry milk
3 mashed medium bananas
1 teaspoon pure vanilla extract
¼ teaspoon sea salt

Directions

1. Thoroughly mix together all the ingredients in a large bowl.
2. This dough will be sticky so place in the refrigerator for about 15 to 20 minutes to chill.
3. Either drop by teaspoonful or roll out dough to ¼ inch thickness using a sheet of wax paper between the dough and the roller. Cut with your favorite cookie cutter.
4. Place on lined baking sheets and bake at 350 degrees for 30 minutes.
5. Turn off oven and leave for about an hour.

Kirby likes lots of banana which makes this is a sticky, wet dough. For a drier dough use less banana or add more flour.

Prep Time: 20 minutes	Cook Time: 30 minutes	
Yields: 100 –2" treats	Calories: 26 each	Calories from fat: 3 each

barkin bacon bites

Kirby very much enjoys these, but then again, what dog can resist bacon. Real bacon bits work fine but baking your own bacon ups it a notch on the nose meter.

The bacon makes it a little harder to use a fancy cookie cutter so I use a simple square cookie cutter. For an intricate cookie cutter you can grind the bacon before adding it. You can also substitute 2 ¾ cup whole wheat flour for the oat flour and brown rice flour.

Ingredients

- 1 ¾ cups oat flour
- 1 cup brown rice flour
- 1 (3 oz.) package real bacon bits (¾ cup cooked, drained bacon)
- 1 cup unsweetened applesauce
- 1 teaspoon ground cinnamon
- 1 large egg

Directions

1. Thoroughly mix together all ingredients in a large bowl. Place in the refrigerator for about 10 minutes to chill which will make it less sticky.
2. Roll out dough to ¼ inch thickness. Cut with your favorite cookie cutter and place on lined baking sheets.
3. Bake at 350 degrees for 20 to 25 minutes until lightly browned on bottoms.
4. Turn off oven and leave for a few hours.

Prep Time: 25 minutes	Cook Time: 25 minutes	
Yields: 76 – 2" squares	Calories: 22 each	Calories from fat: 5 each

blueberry pupcakes

Is your canine companion having a special occasion? A Barkday Party? Furkids coming for a play date? Maybe it's just a glorious summer day worth celebrating? These cute pupcakes are bursting with healthy flavors and antioxidants your dog is craving!

Ingredients

   2 cups oat flour
   2 teaspoons baking powder
   1 teaspoon baking soda
   1 teaspoon pure vanilla extract
   2 cups fresh or frozen blueberries
   3 large eggs
   ½ cup safflower oil
   ½ cup plain Greek yogurt

Directions

1. In a bowl stir together the wet ingredients.
2. In another bowl combine the dry ingredients and add to the wet ingredients stirring just until combined.
3. Evenly spoon mixture into oil sprayed and floured muffin tins.
4. Bake at 350 degrees for 10 to 15 minutes for mini muffins or 22 - 27 minutes for regular size muffins. Muffins are done when toothpick inserted in the center comes out clean.
5. Remove from oven and let cool completely on a baker's rack.

Store individually wrapped in saran wrap in the refrigerator for up to a week. When ready to serve top with some frosting.

Prep Time: 15 minutes	Cook Time: 10 – 27 minutes	
Yields: 12 large, 24 mini	Calories: 179/90 each	Calories from fat: 102/51 each

b'oat bites

Want to make an easy treat? Want to please the finickiest dog? Here's the recipe you need! It all starts with 1 cup of quick cooking oats plus 1 cup of bananas, peaches, apples, or pumpkin. I know you can come up with even more variations than I have. Add a third ingredient if you want to kick them up another notch. This is a healthy treat for the pawrent with little time who wants to pamper their pet with fresh baked morsels of goodness.

And who says you can't share these chewy morsels since they are made with human grade ingredients and nothing else. They can be dairy free, nut free, even gluten free if you use gluten free oats. Yes, I've eaten a few, but honestly these are sweet satisfaction in a bite!

Prep Time: 10 minutes	Cook Time: 10 – 12 minutes	Yields: 30 cookies

banana & oats

2 large mashed bananas
1 cup quick cooking oats

Sizes vary so use enough bananas to equal 1 cup. I've made these with fresh bananas and ripe bananas with the same sweet results.

Calories: 17 each	Calories from fat: 2 each

peaches & oats

1 large pureed peach
1 cup quick cooking oats

Peaches can be pureed in a blender or you can use unsweetened canned peaches.

Calories: 12 each	Calories from fat: 2 each

apples & oats

1 cup cinnamon applesauce
1 cup quick cooking oats

Calories: 14 each	Calories from fat: 2 each

pumpkin & oats

1 cup pure pumpkin
1 cup quick cooking oats

| Calories: 13 each | Calories from fat: 2 each |

Directions

1. Mix together in a medium size bowl. I find it easiest to use my hands to really coat all of the oats.
2. Drop small teaspoonfuls onto lined baking sheet.
3. Bake at 350 degrees for 10 to 12 minutes. Remove to a cooling rack.

The list of healthy ingredients you can add to the oats are endless. Just make sure they are dog friendly: try carob chips, coconut flakes, cranberries, blueberries, bacon, cinnamon, sea salt, parsley, cayenne pepper. These should keep in the refrigerator for about a week but be sure to watch for any mold. They can be frozen for up to three months.

butternut bliss biscuits

Butternut squash provides about one-third of the daily value of vitamin C in every cup and contains vitamins B1, B3, B6, pantothenic acid, and folate. It's a great fall side dish and a perfect ingredient to be used in casseroles. The sweetness of butternut squash also makes it an excellent ingredient for treats.

Ingredients

2 cups oat flour
1 cup cooked butternut squash
½ cup unsweetened applesauce
1 large egg
2 tablespoons maple syrup
1 teaspoon pure vanilla extract
1 ½ teaspoons ground cinnamon
¼ teaspoon sea salt

Directions

1. In a large bowl thoroughly mix all the ingredients.
2. Drop by teaspoonful onto lined baking sheet. These can be placed close together since they won't expand. Lightly sprinkle cinnamon on top of each cookie.
3. Bake at 350 degrees for 30 to 40 minutes or until lightly browned.
4. Remove from the oven to a bakers rack and let cool.

These are great for a treat but even better as an accompaniment biscuit with your dog's meal. They are moist so treat them as a baked good watching for mold.

Prep Time: 10 minutes	Cook Time: 40 minutes	
Yields: 40 – 2" treats	Calories: 26 each	Calories from fat: 4 each

cajun bacun biscuits

Ok, so these aren't really cajun - no hot spicy stuff for the Kirbster! But there is a lot of yummy bacon flavor Kirby loves, actually what dog or human doesn't? These are loaded with sizzling bacon bits and drippings. He's always right next me every second intently watching my every move. Maybe hoping some little bits would fall on the floor? The nose knows!

Ingredients

- 1 (12 oz.) package bacon
- ½ cup bacon drippings
- 2 cups rye flour
- 2 large eggs
- ½ cup dry milk
- ¼ cup water

Directions

1. Cook the bacon until crispy brown.
2. Remove bacon saving the grease and bits.
3. Crumble bacon into a large bowl.
4. Add remaining ingredients except the water and thoroughly mix.
5. Add enough water to make the dough stick together.
6. Roll out ¼ inch thick and cut with cookie cutter.
7. Place on lined baking sheet. These won't rise or spread so you can place them close together.
8. I like to brush an egg wash over the tops before baking just to make them look pastry pretty (that's the French part).
9. Bake at 300 degrees for 15 minutes. These bacony biscuits were actually ~~sizzling~~ singing when I pulled them out!
10. Let cool on baker's rack.

These harden as they cook.

Prep Time: 30 minutes	Cook Time: 15 minutes	
Yields: 98 – 2" squares	Calories: 25 each	Calories from fat: 13 each

carrot pupcakes

Today is Father's Day. I need to call Dad and tell him how much I love him. I need to tell him how I miss him so very much. I need to tell him I wish I could visit with him just one more time. One day he checked into the hospital to have a scheduled surgery on his shoulder. One day he was fine. The next day he was in trouble. He spent almost a month in the ICU. I prayed for a miracle. I waited for a miracle. God took him home on July 23, 2009. Dad's favorite cake was carrot cake. I can't bake one for him but I decided I would bake one for Kirby in Dad's honor. Kirby gives them 5 paws!

Ingredients

- 3 large eggs
- 1/2 cup honey
- ½ cup vanilla Greek yogurt
- 2 cups oat flour
- 2 cups shredded carrots
- 1 teaspoon ground cinnamon
- 1 teaspoon baking powder
- 1 teaspoon baking soda

I was tickled watching Kirby eat one. First he ate the carrot pieces on top, then he licked off the frosting, then he ate the cake. They have just the right amount of sweetness. Actually if he's willing to share, they would be perfect with my morning coffee.

Directions

1. Shred the carrots in a food processor.
2. In a bowl stir together the wet ingredients.
3. In another bowl combine the dry ingredients and add to the wet ingredients stirring just until combined.
4. Evenly spoon mixture into oil sprayed and floured muffin tins filling close to the top.
5. Bake at 350 degrees for 10 - 15 minutes for mini muffins or 20 - 25 minutes for regular size muffins. They're done when a toothpick inserted in the center comes out clean.
6. Let cool completely on baker's rack.

Store individually wrapped in saran wrap in the refrigerator for up to a week. When ready to serve top with some frosting.

Prep Time: 10 minutes	Cook Time: 15-25 minutes	
Yields: 12 large – 24 mini	Calories: 134/67 each	Calories from fat: 20/10 each

Cheeseburgers

cheeseburgers

I love a cheeseburger! My favorite go to recipe is one pound ground beef, one egg, a package of Lipton Onion Soup, and some Worcestershire sauce. Onions are toxic for dogs and I couldn't prove to myself that Worcestershire sauce is safe so this is my dogified version for a cheeseburger treat. I rarely use whole wheat flour in Kirby's treats but I was going for an all American real cheeseburger and who eats a burger with a bun made from rice, oats, or coconut flour? Kirby loves meat so I already knew these would be a tasty hit. Watching him wait in front of the oven as they baked guaranteed they were nose approved.

Ingredients

- ½ lb. ground beef
- ½ cup shredded cheddar cheese
- 2 cups whole wheat flour
- 1 large egg
- ½ cup bone (beef) broth
- ¼ teaspoon garlic powder
- ¼ teaspoon cayenne pepper
- ¼ teaspoon sea salt
- 1 teaspoon blackstrap molasses

Directions

1. Cook and drain the ground beef.
2. In a large bowl combine all the ingredients until thoroughly mixed.
3. Knead the dough a few times to bind it and then roll out on a floured surface ½ inch thick. Cut into shapes with the cutter of your choice. I use a small biscuit cutter since I'm going for the cheeseburger look.
4. Place on lined baking sheets. They won't rise so they can be placed close together. Prick the centers of each treat with a fork to help cook since they are thick.
5. Bake at 350 degrees for 15 minutes. Turn over and cook another 15 minutes. Turn off oven and leave in for about an hour.

Prep Time: 10 minutes	Cook Time: 30 minutes	
Yields: 45 treats	Calories: 37 each	Calories from fat: 8 each

Cheese Nips Kinda

cheese nips kinda

I love to eat cheese nips, a task Kirby quite enjoys helping me with. They probably aren't the healthiest thing for a dog to eat so I decided I needed to make some that were. We do share these a lot!

Butter is cream churned into a solid state containing at least 80% milk fat. You can replace the butter with an equal amount of solid coconut oil which does change the flavor. Either way these are tasty crackers Kirby likes.

Ingredients

   1 cup shredded cheddar cheese
   ½ stick softened unsalted butter
   1 teaspoon sea salt
   1 cup white whole wheat flour
   2 tablespoons ice cold water

Directions

1. In large bowl mix together the cheese, butter, sea salt, and flour.
2. Slowly add the water mixing until the dough forms little balls. Remove from bowl and hand knead until you have a compacted ball.
3. Wrap the ball in saran wrap and refrigerate for thirty minutes.
4. Roll out as thin as possible (1/8-1/16 of an inch thick) on parchment paper.
5. Carefully move the dough and parchment paper to a baking sheet.
6. Use a pizza cutter to perforate small 1" squares. They won't rise so they can stay together.
7. Prick holes in the tops with a toothpick and sprinkle a little sea salt over the top.
8. Bake at 350 degrees for 15 minutes watching for golden edges. Ovens vary so keep an eye on them so they don't burn.
9. Remove immediately and let cool on a baker's rack.

I do always use my stand mixer for this one to save my arm.

You can use any dog friendly flour. I like the white whole wheat flour to allow the cheese to give it a more yellow color. Using rice flour has turned out well too.

Prep Time: 90 minutes	Cook Time: 15 minutes	
Yields: 185 crackers	Calories: 7 each	Calories from fat: 4 each

Chicken Cordon Bleu

chicken cordon bleu

Cordon Bleu literally means 'blue ribbon' and is a name given to distinguished chefs. The original cordon bleu dish was a schnitzel filled with cheese in Switzerland around the 1940's. There are many variations but the popular way to prepare chicken cordon bleu is to butterfly a chicken breast, place a thin slice of ham or prosciutto inside, then place a thin slice of a soft, easily melted cheese. The chicken breast is then rolled up, coated in bread crumbs and deep fried or baked. With Kirby's growing gourmand taste buds I've been delving into gourmet cuisine more and more to give him a true variety of new flavors. He really likes this one!

Ingredients

2 cups oat flour
½ cup cooked chicken
¼ cup (2 slices) shredded Swiss cheese
¼ cup (6 slices) cooked turkey bacon
2 large eggs
¼ teaspoon sea salt
¼ teaspoon cayenne pepper
3 tablespoons extra light olive oil

Directions

1. Shred the chicken and cheese, Crumble the bacon.
2. Thoroughly combine all ingredients in a large bowl. This is crumbly dough so I generously wet my hands, grab a handful, and knead until it is workable dough. Repeat with the remaining dough.
3. Roll out dough to ¼ inch thick and cut out shapes with a cookie cutter. You may have to push the dough together to fix cracks in the cookies but don't worry they will harden and hold together once cooked.
4. Place on lined baking sheet and bake at 350 degrees for 20 minutes.
5. Remove to rack to cool.

Prep Time: 30 minutes	Cook Time: 20 minutes	
Yields: 23 large, 40 small	Calories: 67/38 each	Calories from fat: 30/17 each

coconut catters

Every time I eat coconut ice cream I end up having to share it with Kirby (those sad brown eyes just kill me) so I have wanted to figure out a coconut flavored doggie cookie just for him.

Our two cats, Chelsea and Kaitlyn, very much like these treats hence the name "catters" not to mention the cute whiskers of coconut.

Ingredients

1 ½ cups oat flour
1 ½ cups brown rice flour
1 cup shredded unsweetened coconut
1 teaspoon ground cinnamon
2 large eggs
½ cup coconut milk
2 tablespoons honey

Directions

1. In a large bowl thoroughly mix together all the ingredients.
2. Roll out ¼ inch thick on a floured surface and cut with cookie cutter of choice.
3. Place on lined baking sheet.
4. Bake at 250 degrees for 20 minutes then transfer to a baker's rack to cool or for harder treats turn off oven and leave for about an hour.

Prep Time: 20 minutes	Cook Time: 20 minutes	
Yields: 85 – 2" treats	Calories: 24 each	Calories from fat: 6 each

ezy cheezy

Are you craving something to munch on? Want something good for everyone including the dog? Want something easy? How about just two ingredients? If you said yes then this is what you were looking for.

Ingredients

   2 cups shredded cheese
   4 teaspoons of any flour

Directions

1. Pour cheese into a medium size bowl. Add flour and mix together to coat the cheese. I like using baking flour but any flour will work just fine.
2. Now is the time to throw in any seasonings. I like a pinch of sea salt and some cayenne pepper for a little kick. Make sure any seasoning or herb you choose is dog friendly.
3. Grab a small handful and place on a lined baking sheet. Flatten slightly and make sure there are no loose pieces.
4. Bake at 375 degrees for about 10 minutes or until crispy on the edges.
5. Remove from oven and let cool slightly before removing from the baking sheet.

My favorite is definitely the parmesan cheese whereas Kirby prefers the Colby Jack.

Prep Time: 5 minutes	Cook Time: 10 minutes	
Yields: 6 – 8 treats	Calories: 158/119 each	Calories from fat: 113/84 each

grrreat granola bars

Homemade granola bars are easy to make, freezer friendly, and adaptable to whatever ingredients you want to use. The choices and combinations of ingredients for a granola bar can be endless and dog gone healthy depending on the ingredients chosen. Check my Healthy Ingredients and Safe Herbs & Spices sections to create your own granola bars geared to your pupster.

These are really chewy which Kirby enjoys, however I would recommend having a big bowl of water handy as he takes a few trips to his water fountain. The blackstrap molasses imparts a bittersweet flavor Kirby likes. You can use honey or maple syrup for a sweeter taste. Top them with a dollop of plain Greek yogurt for some probiotic goodness.

Ingredients

2 ½ cups old fashioned oats
½ cup slivered almonds
1 cup (6 oz.) shredded unsweetened coconut
1 ½ teaspoon ground cinnamon
1 ½ teaspoon ground ginger
½ cup ground flax seed
3 tablespoons coconut oil
1/3 cup blackstrap molasses
1/3 cup natural crunchy peanut butter
1 ½ teaspoons pure vanilla extract
¼ teaspoon sea salt
1 ½ cups chopped dried fruit

Directions

1. Preheat the oven to 350 degrees.
2. Line a 9 x 13 pan with aluminum foil leaving a bit of the foil hanging over the edges of the pan to create a 'sling' so you can lift the granola out of the pan once baked. Do not use wax paper which I found the hard way will stick to the granola. Spray the foil with olive oil or a non-stick cooking spray.
3. Finely chop the almonds with ½ cup of the oats in a food processor.
4. Toss the oatmeal, almonds, and coconut together in a large bowl and then spread on a baking sheet and bake for 10 to 12 minutes, stirring occasionally, until lightly browned.
5. Transfer this mixture back to the mixing bowl and stir in the flax seed, cinnamon, ginger and salt.
6. Add the dried fruit. I use cranberries, cherries, and blueberries. I also chop the fruit into smaller pieces based on Kirby's preference but this is optional.

7. Reduce the oven temperature to 300 degrees F.
8. Place the coconut oil, molasses, peanut butter, and vanilla in a small saucepan and bring to a boil over medium heat constantly stirring. Cook for about a minute and then slowly pour it over the toasted oatmeal mixture.
9. Now you need to mix it all together until it's completely coated. Using the side of a large stiff rubber spatula cut through the mix over and over while rotating the bowl. This breaks up all the clumps of moistened ingredients so that any remaining dry ingredients can be incorporated.
10. Spoon into the prepared pan. Oil or wet your hands and press the mixture down firmly.
11. Bake for 25 minutes, then reduce the temperature to 250 degrees and bake for another 15 minutes until light golden brown.
12. Remove from the oven and press down using a spatula. They'll seem like they are too soft but they will set once completely cooled.
13. Let them cool for about 20 minutes then remove from the pan using the foil sling as handles. Gently cut the bars or squares with a very sharp knife but don't separate them until they are fully cooled which will take 2 to 3 hours. If the bars seem crumbly, chilling them in the refrigerator for 30 minutes sometimes helps set the "glue".

Wrap bars individually in plastic wrap as soon as possible so they don't dry out and crumble. They will keep in the fridge or at room temperature for up to 1 week. You can place the wrapped bars in a large freezer bag and freeze for up to three months. They will thaw within an hour or so.

Overall, the bars will stay together. I store the crumbly bits in an airtight container in the fridge to toss over his dinners.

Prep Time: 25 minutes	Cook Time: 60 minutes	
Yields: 35 squares	Calories: 140 each	Calories from fat: 53 each

Green Eggs & Ham

green eggs & ham

> "Do you like green eggs and ham?
> I do not like them, Sam-I-am.
> I do not like green eggs and ham."

Sam-I-am clearly did not care for green eggs and ham, but if he had a dog, that dog would gobble up these green eggs & ham treats and beg for more! Kirby rarely gets to eat pork (bacon excluded) since it's such a fatty protein so he really enjoys this taste changer. Does Kirby like the beautiful green color? The healthy serving of spinach in each bite? The delicious aroma of ham and cheese? OK, it's the flavors!

You can change the ingredient ratios - too much spinach? Use just a cup and add an extra ½ cup bread crumbs. Either way, feel free to have a few yourself. They are delicious made with human grade ingredients!

Ingredients

- 1 ½ cups chopped fresh or frozen spinach
- 1 ½ cups chopped cooked ham
- 2 cups unseasoned bread crumbs
- 6 beaten large eggs
- ¼ cup parmesan cheese
- 1/3 cup shredded cheddar cheese
- ½ cup extra light olive oil
- ½ teaspoon sea salt

Directions

1. Thoroughly mix all the ingredients in a large bowl.
2. Scoop spoonfuls and place on a lined baking sheet. They won't rise so you can place them close together.
3. Bake at 350 degrees for 30 minutes or until lightly browned around the bottom edges.

These are a soft treat so keep an eye out for mold.

Prep Time: 15 minutes	Cook Time: 30 minutes	
Yields: 76 treats	Calories: 42 each	Calories from fat: 23 each

Harvest Pumpkin Balls

harvest pumpkin balls

Fall is the time to stock up on canned pure pumpkin which is an amazing ingredient for dogs. Constipated? A little pumpkin can help. Runny stools? A little pumpkin can help. Upset tummy or trying to transition to a new food? Again, a little pumpkin can help!

This recipe is not only tasty but chock full of incredibly healthy ingredients for sensitive tummies. Pumpkin is packed with large quantities of vitamin A for resistance to infections, improve night vision and keep the body's membranes healthy, potassium for good blood pressure, iron for healthy blood, and roughage to help digestion.

Ingredients

- 2 cups oat flour
- 1 large egg
- 1 cup pure pumpkin
- 2 tablespoons honey
- 2 teaspoons ground flax seed
- ¼ teaspoon ground cinnamon
- ¼ teaspoon sea salt

Directions

1. Thoroughly mix together all the ingredients in a medium size bowl.
2. Scoop out balls with a cookie scooper and let them chill in the refrigerator for about 10 minutes. Then cut them in half with a sharp knife and roll into smaller balls.
3. Place close together on lined baking sheet and bake at 350 degrees for 20 minutes.
4. Remove from the oven and let cool.

If you don't want to spend the time forming the balls, use a spatula to smooth out the mixture on a lined baking sheet. When halfway baked, score with a pizza cutter. Watch the cooking time as the thinner they are the faster they will bake.

These treats have a crispy outside with a soft, moist center which means they will mold like any baked good.

Prep Time: 30 minutes	Cook Time: 20 minutes	
Yields: 44 large / 88 small	Calories: 23/12 each	Calories from fat: 4/2 each

lamb nuggets

Crispy on the outside, moist on the inside, these tasty morsels of potato filled with succulent lamb are truly like nuggets of gold. They'll have your dog doing every trick he knows. So go ahead, treat him like the pampered pooch he deserves to be.

Ingredients

2 cups potato flour
¼ cup dry milk
1 cup cooked, drained ground lamb
1 tablespoon dried parsley
¼ teaspoon dried rosemary
2 large eggs
2 cups chicken broth

Directions

1. Combine the flour, dry milk, parsley, and rosemary in a medium size bowl.
2. Mix in the lamb and add the eggs.
3. Stir in the broth.
4. Using a scoop, or your hands, form small balls and place on lined baking sheet.
5. Bake at 350 degrees for up to 30 minutes or until bottoms are lightly browned. Turn off the oven and leave in for about thirty minutes.

Kirby LOVES these expensive nuggets so I try to make them as often as my budget allows.

Prep Time: 30 minutes	Cook Time: 30 minutes	
Yields: 82 – 1" treats	Calories: 40 each	Calories from fat: 12 each

liver lover's meaty bones

These are one of the "Kirby's Barkery" treats we used to sell at the festivals. We had samples of three different treats for taste testing so it always amused me how many people didn't care for the liver smell until their dogs begged for them. Let me just say we sold quite a few 8 oz. bags!

To release any toxins stored in the meat and remove some of the pungent liver smell, you can place the liver in a covered container with 2 tablespoons of apple cider vinegar and refrigerate overnight before making this recipe.

Ingredients

½ lb. calf liver
1 ¾ cups brown rice flour
1 ¾ cups oat flour
1 ¼ cups shredded cheddar cheese
1 large egg

Directions

1. Puree the liver.
2. Add the remaining ingredients and thoroughly mix.
3. Roll out on a floured surface and cut out with cookie cutter.
4. Place on lined baking sheet and bake at 275 degrees for 15 minutes.
5. Turn off oven and leave in overnight.

Be sure to immediately rinse anything that comes into contact with the liver or you will have a stuck-on mess!

Prep Time: 15 minutes	Cook Time: 15 minutes	
Yields: 120 – 3" treats	Calories: 22 each	Calories from fat: 6 each

liver pate' bites

Crispy on the outside, soft and chewy on the inside. We all know liver is a favorite among dogs but did you know many like the sweet nutty taste of barley?

Can't stand the smell of liver? A trick is to place it in a covered container with about 2 tablespoons of apple cider vinegar and refrigerate overnight. This will release any toxins that were stored in the meat and remove some of the pungent liver smell.

Ingredients

 1 cup calf liver
 ½ cup bone (beef) broth or chicken stock
 2 ½ cups barley flour
 2 tablespoons dried parsley
 3 tablespoons extra light olive oil
 1 large egg

Directions

1. Puree the liver with the broth or stock.
2. Add the remaining ingredients and thoroughly mix.
3. Make small balls with a cookie scoop or your hands.
4. Place on lined baking sheet and bake at 350 degrees for 25 minutes.
5. Remove to cooling rack.

These are soft on the inside so treat as with any bakery product watching for mold and spoilage.

Be sure to immediately rinse anything that comes into contact with the liver or you will have a stuck-on mess!

Prep Time: 15 minutes	Cook Time: 25 minutes	
Yields: 52 – 1" balls	Calories: 41 each	Calories from fat: 11 each

Milk Bones

milk bones

Milk Bones dog treats have been around for as long as I can remember. I see boxes every time I'm in Wal-Mart or the grocery store. The main ingredients are wheat flour, wheat bran, meat and bone meal, milk, and beef fat so this is my version which I think is a tad healthier and much cheaper.

Ingredients

- 3 cups whole wheat flour
- ½ cup dry milk
- 1 teaspoon sea salt
- 1 cup bone (beef) broth
- 1 large egg

Directions

1. In a large bowl combine all the ingredients and thoroughly mix.
2. Place in the refrigerator for about 15 minutes to chill.
3. Roll dough out to ½ inch thick and cut with bone cutters.
4. Place on lined baking sheet. These won't spread so they can be placed close together.
5. Prick each treat with fork tines to allow steam to escape. Since these are thick this will prevent the bottom from burning before the center has cooked.
6. I brush the tops with an egg wash to make them shiny which is totally optional.
7. Bake at 325 degrees for 50 minutes.
8. Remove to rack to cool.

These will be hard on the outside yet slightly chewy inside. For really hard treats, turn off the oven and leave them in overnight.

Prep Time: 20 minutes	Cook Time: 50 minutes	
Yields: 70 treats	Calories: 22 each	Calories from fat: 2 each

mississippi mud puppies

I had a "Mississippi Mud Puppy" the other day. Yum, yum, yum! It got me to thinking why not make something like this for Kirby except, since he can't eat chocolate which is my true love, use liver, which is his true love. You really should try the human version and of course my dogified delicious version for your pups.

Ingredients

½ lb. calf liver
2 cups oat flour
2 large eggs
1 cup dried cranberries
¼ cup ground flax seed

Directions

1. Chop up the cranberries in a food processor using a little of the flour for the stickiness.
2. Puree the liver in a blender or food processor.
3. Thoroughly combine all the ingredients.
4. Using a spatula, spread out the mixture on an oiled foil covered jelly roll or baking sheet to about ½ inch thick. Rinsing the spatula under hot water will help it stick less and spread better. (To make individual cookies, drop by teaspoonfuls and flatten.)
5. Bake at 350 degrees for 40 minutes. I wanted a chewy texture but you can cook another 10 to 15 minutes and then turn off the oven to achieve hard crunchy treats.
6. Remove using the foil as a sling to a baker's rack to cool.
7. Once cooled peel away the foil and cut into small squares with a pizza cutter or knife.

I'm not tasting these because I simply cannot stand the taste of liver but Kirby loves liver, loves these, and loves me!

When storing be sure to check for any mold as these are on the moist side.

Be sure to immediately rinse anything that comes into contact with the liver or you will have a stuck-on mess!

Prep Time: 20 minutes	Cook Time: 40 minutes	
Yields: 144 – 1" squares	Calories: 10 each	Calories from fat: 3 each

pawsome pumpkin pupcakes

I love to bake, and with fall in the air, there are so many yummy vegetables just waiting to be tried. Pumpkin is always at the top of the list with cans of pure pumpkin loading the shelves and fresh pumpkins sitting in bins. I'm lazy so I use canned pumpkin (never pumpkin pie which is loaded with unnecessary sugars) but if you really want fresh then choose sugar pumpkins. Kirby just loves some pumpkin which has a naturally sweet flavor and is so good for a dog's digestive system so I stock up when it's available.

Ingredients

  1 cup pure pumpkin
  ¼ cup honey
  ½ cup unsweetened applesauce
  2 large eggs
  ½ teaspoon pure vanilla extract
  ¼ cup safflower oil or vegetable oil
  1 cup oat flour
  1 ½ teaspoons baking powder
  1 teaspoon baking soda
  1/8 teaspoon sea salt
  1 teaspoon ground cinnamon
  1/8 teaspoon ground ginger

Directions

1. In a bowl stir together the wet ingredients.
2. In another bowl combine the dry ingredients and add to the wet ingredients stirring just until combined.
3. Fill oil sprayed and floured muffin tins 3/4 full as they will rise a little.
4. Bake at 350 degrees for 40 minutes or until a toothpick inserted into the center comes out clean.
5. Let cool.

Store individually wrapped in saran wrap in the refrigerator for up to a week. When ready to serve top with Pumpkin Cream Cheese Frosting.

Prep Time: 15 minutes	Cook Time: 40 minutes	
Yields: 12 large, 24 mini	Calories: 115/58 each	Calories from fat: 53/26 each

peanut butter paws

This is our third "Kirby's Barkery" dog treat we made for the festivals using cute paw shaped cookie cutters. Peanut butter is always a popular taste so these sold out quickly.

Ingredients

1 ½ cups oat flour
½ cup natural peanut butter
¼ cup dry milk
¼ cup water
1 tablespoon blackstrap molasses
1 large egg

Directions

1. In a large bowl combine all the ingredients and thoroughly mix.
2. Place in the refrigerator for about 15 minutes to chill.
3. Roll dough out to ½ inch thick and cut with bone cutters.
4. Place on lined baking sheet. These won't spread so they can be placed close together.
5. Prick each treat with fork tines to allow steam to escape. Since these are thick this will prevent the bottom from burning before the center has cooked.
6. I brush the tops with an egg wash to make them shiny which is totally optional.
7. Bake at 350 degrees for 40 to 50 minutes.
8. Turn off oven and leave in overnight.

Prep Time: 20 minutes	Cook Time: 40 minutes	
Yields: 70 – 3" treats	Calories: 21 each	Calories from fat: 10 each

pesto puppers

I have an herb garden and I always know what to do with all that basil. Maybe it's because I'm half Italian or maybe it's just because I love the flavors. I love pesto on pasta, salads, pizza, fish, you name it, pesto can make it better! Pesto is super easy to make and it's packed with health benefits like heart-healthy mono-unsaturated fatty acids, iron, and vitamin C.

The other night I was starving for a snack and all I could come up with was smearing some pesto on wheat thins. Turns out I really enjoyed it as did Kirby which got me to thinking about a pesto dog treat. Kirby likes savory flavors, it would be healthy, and yes my mind does always lead back to dog treats.

Ingredients

1 ½ cups oat flour
1 cup brown rice flour
½ cup Greek yogurt
1 large egg
¼ cup unsweetened applesauce
½ teaspoon pure vanilla extract
2 tablespoons basil pesto (recipe follows)
½ teaspoon baking soda
½ teaspoon sea salt

Directions

1. In a large bowl thoroughly mix together all of the ingredients.
2. Place bowl in the refrigerator for about fifteen minutes to chill.
3. Roll out the dough to ½ inch thick and cut out shapes with a cookie cutter or biscuit cutter.
4. Place on a lined baking sheet and bake at 375 degrees for 8 to 10 minutes or until edges brown. At this point the outside is crispy while the inside is still soft. You can turn off the oven and leave them in for about an hour to harden.
5. Remove and place on cooling rack.

These are crispy on the outside but soft on the inside so treat as any bakery product.

Prep Time: 30 minutes	Cook Time: 10 minutes	
Yields: 38 – 2" rounds	Calories: 43 each	Calories from fat: 13 each

basil pesto

This is my basic pesto recipe which is really called "pistou" due to the lack of nuts. Get creative to find the perfect flavors for your own pesto. Swap out the basil with spinach or parsley. I've tried it with cilantro and didn't like the flavor but many do so it is an option. Replace the parmesan cheese with pecorino, romano or feta cheese.

A true pesto includes pine nuts but I'm leery of them being dog friendly so I stopped using them a long time ago and I really don't miss them. You could add ¼ cup almonds or sunflower seeds.

Ingredients

    2 cups fresh basil leaves
    2 garlic cloves
    ¼ cup parmesan cheese
    ¼ teaspoon lemon juice
    ¼ teaspoon sea salt
    ¼ cup extra light olive oil

Directions

1. Finely chop the garlic and place in the food processor.
2. Add the basil leaves, parmesan cheese, lemon juice, and sea salt. Blend just until the basil is finely chopped.
3. Slowly drizzle in the olive oil while the machine is running to create an emulsion.

Pesto will keep in the refrigerator up to two weeks. You can freeze it in small freezer safe containers, use ice cube trays or a cookie scoop to make small balls by placing on a lined baking sheet and freezing.

Prep Time: 10 minutes	Cook Time: None	
Yields: 1/2 cup	Calories: 79 per tbsp.	Calories from fat: 71 per tbsp.

Pumpkin Cran Muffins

pumpkin cran muffins

Pumpkin, cranberries, cinnamon, seriously what's a pup not to love? These are pawsitively pawfect for that special occasion like a barkday or a puppy play date or when you just want to show some extra appreciation for all that unconditional love you've been getting every day.

These muffins have a chewy texture. Serve them plain or add a dollop of cream cheese on top with a sprinkle of cinnamon.

Ingredients

- 1 cup pure pumpkin
- 1 cup unsweetened applesauce
- 2 tablespoons honey
- 1 large egg
- 1 cup oat flour
- 2 teaspoons baking powder
- 3 teaspoons ground cinnamon
- ¼ teaspoon ground ginger
- ½ cup dried cranberries

Directions

1. In a bowl stir together the wet ingredients.
2. In another bowl combine the dry ingredients and add to the wet ingredients stirring just until combined.
3. Evenly spoon mixture into oiled muffin tins.
4. Bake at 350 degrees for 30 minutes in a mini muffin pan or for 40 minutes in a regular muffin pan.
5. Let them cool a few minutes then remove to a baker's rack to completely cool.

Store individually wrapped in saran wrap in the refrigerator for up to a week. When ready to serve top with some frosting.

They should be treated as any moist baked good by watching out for mold.

Prep Time: 10 minutes	Cook Time: 30 minutes	
Yields: 12 large, 24 mini	Calories: 66/33 each	Calories from fat: 8/4 each

puppermint patties

These cookies have just enough mint to freshen that doggie breath and the aroma that fills the kitchen while they bake is oh so divine. Kirby gives them four paws up!

Ingredients

- 3 cups oat flour
- ¼ cup dry milk
- ½ cup chicken stock
- 1 large egg
- ½ teaspoon baking powder
- 2 tablespoons chopped fresh mint or ¼ teaspoon peppermint oil
- ¼ cup dried parsley

Directions

1. Thoroughly mix together all the ingredients adding a little water if the dough is too dry.
2. Roll out the dough to ¼ inch thickness and cut out shapes with cookie cutters.
3. Place on lined baking sheet. They can be close together since they won't spread. Brush with an egg wash if desired for a little shine.
4. Bake at 350 degrees for 30 minutes.
5. Remove to baker's rack to cool.

Prep Time: 10 minutes	Cook Time: 30 minutes	
Yields: 40 treats	Calories: 30 each	Calories from fat: 5 each

pupperoni pizza pies

Kirby didn't like my first pizza recipe concoction. So in the second batch I used less rye flour which has a slightly sour taste, added oat flour and discarded the rosemary. He likes them but not a favorite. Funny thing is if I offer him one he will sniff it and walk away. If I break one open and offer it he gobbles it up. I'm curious to know what other dogs think...

Ingredients

1 3/4 cups rye flour or whole wheat flour
1 cup oat flour
½ cup (3.5 oz.) shredded pepperoni
½ cup parmesan cheese
1 (6 oz.) can tomato paste
¼ teaspoon ground oregano
¼ teaspoon dried parsley
1 large egg
¼ cup water

Directions

1. Thoroughly mix all ingredients in a large bowl.
2. This is a dry dough so I like to work small batches at a time. Grab a handful and knead then roll out to a ¼ inch thick and cut with favorite cookie cutter or use a pizza cutter to cut small squares.
3. Place on lined baking sheet. They will not spread so they can be placed close together.
4. Bake at 350 degrees for up to 20 minutes or until golden brown on bottom. Let cool on a baker's rack or leave in the turned off oven for about an hour.

Prep Time: 20 minutes	Cook Time: 20 minutes	
Yields: 100 – 1" treats	Calories: 21 each	Calories from fat: 8 each

sweet potato puffs

These puffs of sweet goodness are especially good for dogs who may have trouble chewing hard treats.

Ingredients

1 small sweet potato
1 medium ripe banana
½ cup unsweetened applesauce
2 cups brown rice flour
¼ cup ground flax seed
1 large egg

Directions

1. Cook sweet potato in microwave for roughly 3 to 4 minutes to soften.
2. Cut in half and scoop out the sweet potato.
3. Mash together the sweet potato and banana.
4. Add the remaining ingredients and mix thoroughly.
5. Use a small cookie scoop to make 1 inch balls and place on lined baking sheet.
6. Flatten each ball with a wet fork. (If you want to cut out cookie shapes then add more flour to make dough less sticky and easier to work with).
7. Bake at 300 degrees for 30 minutes. Let cool.

They will keep a few days in an airtight container in the refrigerator. Watch for mold and throw away at the first sign.

Prep Time: 20 minutes	Cook Time: 30 minutes	
Yields: 78 – 1" treats	Calories: 21 each	Calories from fat: 3 each

tasty tuna treats

I wanted to make Kirby a special new treat since he would be boarding for the first time over the next few days. Searching my pantry I discovered I was out of quite a few ingredients. Message to self: take a trip to the grocery store soon. Since I didn't have time to run to the grocery store I thought I would improvise with what I had and hope for the best. Fortunately Kirby gave it four paws up! Seriously I think there's a cat inside that dog!

Ingredients

- 2 (5 oz.) cans tuna fish
- 1 tablespoon salmon oil*
- 1 ½ cups spelt flour**
- ½ cup parmesan cheese
- 1 large egg
- ½ cup water

Directions

1. Drain the tuna, saving the liquid.
2. Puree the tuna with the oil.
3. Take the saved liquid and add enough water to make ½ cup.
4. Thoroughly combine all of the ingredients in a medium bowl.
5. Using a spatula spread out the mixture on a greased or parchment lined jelly roll pan. (If you really want to cut cookie shapes then you can reduce or omit the water or add more flour until you have a better consistency to work with)
6. Bake at 350 degrees for 20 minutes. Turn off the oven and let sit for another 20 minutes with the door slightly ajar.
7. Remove to cutting board. Slice into small pieces using a pizza cutter.

* You can substitute extra light olive oil. I like to use salmon oil which is great for his skin and coat.

** You can use oat flour or whole wheat flour.

Prep Time: 15 minutes	Cook Time: 20 minutes	
Yields: 100+ 1" treats	Calories: 12 each	Calories from fat: 4 each

the elvis biscuit (A big hunk o love)

Remember the King of rock and roll? That voice, that smirkish grin, those hips. Elvis Presley rocked my world so thinking about something special to make for Valentine's Day I immediately thought about his peanut butter and banana sandwich fried in butter. The story is his mother, Gladys, originally made this sandwich Elvis would request over and over throughout his life. The "Elvis Sandwich" sounds like a really gross concoction but until you've eaten one you have no idea how scrumptious it truly is. Trust me, this culinary disaster is deliciously divine!

If you aren't from the South you may be wondering why I add the bacon. Of course that greatly pleases Kirby but rumor has it Elvis loved to add a few slices of bacon for a little crunchy texture.

Ingredients

- 2 cups whole wheat flour or oat flour
- 2 large mashed bananas
- ½ cup natural peanut butter
- 1 (2.5 oz.) bag real bacon bits
- 1 large egg

Directions

1. Mash the bananas in a large bowl.
2. Add the remaining ingredients and mix until thoroughly combined.
3. This is a soft, sticky dough so let it chill in the refrigerator for about 15 minutes.
4. Roll out ¼ inch thick on a floured surface and cut with cookie cutters.
5. Place on a lined baking sheet. They can be placed close together since they won't rise.
6. Brush tops with egg wash (optional) and bake at 350 degrees for about 20 to 25 minutes or until bottoms turn light brown.
7. Remove to a baker's rack to cool. For harder treats, leave in the turned off oven a few hours or overnight.

Prep Time: 20 minutes	Cook Time: 25 minutes	
Yields: 55 – 3" treats	Calories: 45 each	Calories from fat: 20 each

the great plumpkin

The other day I came home from work to a smelly mess. Apparently Kirby had an upset stomach with a nasty bout of diarrhea which I am attributing to the Vienna sausages a friend shared with him the night before. His eyes looked good so I knew he didn't need a visit to his vet. After cleaning up him and the mess in his playroom, I turned to Google. Three ingredients kept popping up as I searched for a home remedy. Pumpkin, cayenne pepper, and probiotics (yogurt).

That night when preparing his evening meal I chose white fish, pumpkin with a dash of cayenne pepper and plain Greek yogurt. Kirby ate the fish, then the yogurt, then the pumpkin in that order. He devoured every morsel so I decided to create a treat using these ingredients.

Ingredients

1 ½ cups brown rice flour
¾ cup pure pumpkin
3 tablespoons plain Greek yogurt
¼ teaspoon cayenne pepper

Directions

1. In a medium bowl thoroughly mix all the ingredients.
2. Roll out ¼ inch thick on a floured surface and cut out shapes with cookie cutters. Place on a lined baking sheet.
3. Bake at 350 degrees for 23 - 25 minutes or until lightly browned on the bottom.
4. Remove to a baker's rack to cool.

These have a chewy texture. For crisper cookies, turn off the oven and leave in for a few hours or overnight.

I am pleased to say Kirby was ok the next day. Home remedies really do work but if you have any doubts, always check with your veterinarian first. If diarrhea persists, or the dog becomes lethargic, or begins vomiting, a visit to the veterinarian is imperative. One phone call only takes a few minutes.

Prep Time: 20 minutes	Cook Time: 25 minutes	
Yields: 56 – 2" treats	Calories: 17 each	Calories from fat: 1 each

the kirbylicious barkday cake

I concocted this yummy cake especially for Kirby's 4th barkday. It just amazes me how the time has flown by. He still acts like a puppy with his energy and silly antics. This sweet boy loves meat so I knew that would be a must have ingredient. We had just smoked a ham earlier in the week and, since I had a bag of bacon bits, this was pretty easy to come up with. This is an extra special treat because ham is a fatty meat he rarely gets to eat.

Ingredients

2 cups oat flour
2 teaspoons baking powder
1 teaspoon baking soda
3 large eggs
1 ½ cups shredded cooked ham
¼ cup unsweetened applesauce
¼ cup extra light olive oil
1 teaspoon ground cinnamon
1 tablespoon maple syrup

Directions

1. In a bowl stir together the wet ingredients.
2. In another bowl combine the dry ingredients and add to the wet ingredients stirring just until combined.
3. Pour into silicone molds, greased muffin tins, or greased cake pan.
4. Bake at 350 degrees for 30 to 35 minutes. Cake is done when toothpick inserted in center comes out clean.
5. Remove from oven and let cool for about 15 minutes before removing to cool on a baker's rack.
6. Frost with Bacon Cream Cheese Frosting.

Prep Time: 20 minutes	Cook Time: 35 minutes	
Yields: 12 large, 24 mini	Calories: 151/76 each	Calories from fat: 74/37 each

turkey n rye meaty bones

Have some leftover turkey? Then you must give this recipe a try! These were one of the first recipes I created for "Kirby's Barkery" which we sold at a few festivals and the local co-op with great success. With a full time job, I just couldn't find the time to continue that endeavor which is lucky for your pups because now you can bake them in your own home.

How good are they? Every time I laid these out with several other popular "store bought" treats Kirby and every foster always picked them first. Indulge your pups with a tasty treat that won't last long!

Ingredients

- 2 ½ cups rye flour
- 1 ½ cups shredded roasted turkey
- ½ cup dried cranberries
- 1 large egg
- ½ cup dry milk
- ½ cup chicken stock
- 2 teaspoons ground flax seed
- 2 teaspoons dried parsley
- 2 tablespoons extra light olive oil

Directions

1. In a large bowl mix together all the ingredients until fully combined.
2. Lightly knead and then roll out ¼ inch thick.
3. Cut out shapes with a bone cookie cutter.
4. Bake at 275 degrees on lined baking sheets for 10 minutes.
5. Turn off the oven and leave them in the oven for one hour.

Prep Time: 15 minutes	Cook Time: 20 minutes	
Yields: 36 – 2" bones	Calories: 48 each	Calories from fat: 14 each

baked grain free treats

These grain free dog treat recipes are designed for dogs that suffer from grain allergies but still deserve a tasty treat. It's also good to treat with grain free if you're trying to help your dog lose weight.

All American Apple Pie	103
Banana Maple Crisps	105
Barkin Bird Bones	107
Cheesy Mashed Taters	109
Holy Mackerel	111
Honey Roasted Chickpeas	113
Peanut Butter & Jelly Sandwiches	114
Savory Beef Bits	115

all american apple pie

Fall means kitchens are filled with scents of apple pie, pumpkin pie and pecan pie. All of which Kirby would love a tasty bite, no he would love a slice. Ok he probably does get a bit now and then but I'm telling you, he has his drool look down pat! My apple pie has a lot of sugar so these were easy enough to whip up to satisfy his yearning with just a few ingredients. Make them fancy using cookie cutters or make them simple by rolling into little balls using a fork to press them down. Either way is tasty!

Ingredients

- 1 cup brown rice flour
- ½ cup coconut flour
- 1 large (1½ cups) red apple
- 2 teaspoons ground cinnamon
- ¼ teaspoon sea salt
- 1 teaspoon pure vanilla extract
- 1 large egg
- ¼ cup apple cider
- 2 tablespoons honey (optional)

Directions

1. Peel, core, and finely chop the apple.
2. In a large bowl thoroughly mix all of the ingredients and roll out about ¼ inch to ½ inch thick. This dough is sticky but pliable so I recommend either rolling between two sheets of wax paper or using a little extra flour.
3. Cut out shapes and place on lined baking sheet. Since these are thick prick centers with a fork to allow steam to release. Even easier is to just roll into small balls, place on parchment paper and flatten with a fork.
4. Bake at 350 degrees for 12-15 minutes until bottoms are golden brown.
5. Remove to a baker's rack to cool.

You can substitute 1½ cups white whole wheat flour for the brown rice flour and coconut flour.

Prep Time: 15 minutes	Cook Time: 10 minutes	
Yields: 34 – 2" rounds	Calories: 35 each	Calories from fat: 4 each

Banana Maple Crisps

banana maple crisps

I love Maple Banana Bread which is so delish! The aroma, the texture, the flavor, I thought why not turn it into a dog treat. Trying to decide what flour to use I finally decided to just leave it out to see what would happen. Bananas work well as a replacement for eggs to bind together but to really make the mixture stay together I used ground flax seed in place of the vegetable oil. It worked out quite well for a crispy, chewy treat which, by the way, Kirby has been forced to share with the human members of his pack.

Ingredients

- 3 medium ripe bananas
- ½ cup ground flax seed
- 1 tablespoon maple syrup

Directions

1. Mash the bananas in a small bowl. Add the flax seed and thoroughly mix together. Stir in the maple syrup.
2. Drop by teaspoonful onto a parchment paper lined baking sheet and press flat.
3. Bake at 300 degrees for 25 minutes and then turn over. Bake another 10 minutes or until the edges are brown and the tops are hard.
4. Turn off the oven and leave in for about an hour to really crisp up.

The smaller and thinner, the less time it will take to bake. Sometimes it's easier to spread out the mixture on the baking sheet and cut into small squares halfway through the baking using a pizza cutter so you can snap the pieces apart once cooled.

Prep Time: 5 minutes	Cook Time: 35 minutes	
Yields: 22 large treats	Calories: 30 each	Calories from fat: 7 each

Barkin Bird Bones

barkin bird bones

I never let Kirby eat chicken bones. I don't care if they are raw or not, it just seems like an accident waiting to happen. Then one day I was making a pot of chicken stock and a light bulb went off. Just as I was about to trash the carcass I decided why not grind it up for some kind of treat since dogs do need the calcium found in bones.

Which is exactly what I did. The bones, the liver, the heart, the gizzards and the neck all went into my Ninja food processor. What I had was a very soft mixture. I gave Kirby a taste which he greedily lapped up so I forged ahead. I wanted 100% .pure chicken bone but over time I've added spices and herbs to up the flavor. If you don't make your own chicken stock, you can use the carcass from a baked or rotisserie chicken. Any bird bones, including turkey and duck, should be easy to grind once they have boiled in water for several hours.

Ingredients

    ground leftover chicken carcass
    ground neck and organ meat

Directions

To make bark:
1. Roll out the mixture very thin between two pieces of wax paper. Remove the top sheet and cut into sizes that will fit in your dehydrator.
2. Place the pieces along with the bottom sheet on the racks. When the top side of the mixture is dry, turn over and toss the wax paper. This can also be done in the oven at the lowest temperature.

To make treats:
1. Place the batter in a baggie, snip a corner, and squeeze out log shapes.
2. Bake at 350 degrees for 30 minutes. Turn off oven and leave the treats until they have hardened. If you really want to make shapes with cookie cutters, add some flour to make the dough easier to manage otherwise they will lose their shape.

Be aware that although excess calcium is not dangerous for adult dogs, large amounts can lead to constipation so feed these sparingly.

Prep Time: 10 minutes	Cook Time: 30 minutes	
Yields: unknown	Calories: unknown	Calories from fat: unknown

cheesy mashed taters

Movie night and you want something savory to munch on? If you're cutting back on the chips and you're tired of popcorn, try this easy, cheesy treat you can share with your pups. The taste will remind you of a loaded baked potato but in a finger food friendly kind of way.

Ingredients

- 2 cups instant mashed potato flakes
- 2 cups water
- ½ teaspoon sea salt
- ¾ cup almond milk
- 3 tablespoons plain Greek yogurt
- 1 cup shredded cheddar cheese
- ½ cup cooked crumbled bacon

Directions

1. In a medium pot bring the water and sea salt to a boil. Remove from heat and stir in the almond milk, yogurt and potato flakes.
2. Pour into a large bowl and mix in the cheddar cheese and bacon.
3. Spoon the mixture onto a lined baking sheet and spread evenly about ¼ inch thick.
4. Bake at 400 degrees for 45 - 50 minutes until the bottom and edges are browned and crispy.
5. Remove and let cool. Cut squares using a knife or pizza cutter.

I don't think they're as good the day after as they lose their crispness. Luckily we don't ever have any leftovers but they can be stored in an air tight container in the refrigerator for a few days.

Prep Time: 10 minutes	Cook Time: 50 minutes	
Yields: 70 treats	Calories: 26 each	Calories from fat: 16 each

Holy Mackerel

holy mackerel

I am a Christian who believes this little dog is a gift from God. Therefore, I knew I needed to concoct a few fish treats for the Kirbster in celebration of Easter. Kirby loved these so much he was very vocal about wanting more until I finally had to say no more.

The Fish is an important symbol serving as the catalyst for the disciples to recognize the resurrected Jesus beside the shore. It was also a symbol for early Christians because the Greek word -- "fish" -- forms an acrostic consisting of the first letters of the phrase "Jesus Christ, the Son of God." In essence the fish was the means by which both Jesus and early Christians were recognized and has become a long-standing favorite rooted deep in history and tradition. The Jesus Fish, or Ichthus, has become a proud symbol of faith and belief.

Ingredients

- 1 (15 oz.) can mackerel
- 1 ½ cups instant mashed potato flakes
- 2 beaten large eggs
- 1 tablespoon lemon juice
- 2 tablespoon dried parsley
- ¼ teaspoon sea salt

Directions

1. Drain the mackerel, saving the juice.
2. Break apart and carefully remove, or mash, the spine bones.
3. In a medium bowl thoroughly mix together all of the ingredients. Add just enough of the mackerel juice to help the ingredients stick together.
4. Shape into small balls or patties if preferred. The dryness causes them to be a little hard to form but they will bake to a perfect crunchy on the outside, soft on the inside morsel. It's easiest to use a small cookie scooper.
5. Arrange on a lined baking sheet.
6. Bake at 350 degrees for 20 minutes.
7. Remove to a baker's rack to cool.

These are soft on the inside, so like any bakery product, keep an eye out for mold.

Prep Time: 20 minutes	Cook Time: 20 minutes	
Yields: 40 balls	Calories: 38 each	Calories from fat: 19 each

Honey Roasted Chickpeas

honey roasted chickpeas

Chickpeas and garbanzo beans are the same thing so look for either but always try to go for organic. Watch out for salt too since sea salt is the only kind considered safe for dogs. The brand I use contains only water and seaweed, another healthy ingredient for dogs.

The texture of roasted chickpeas is surprisingly crispy and crunchy just like potato chips which makes them a great low fat healthy snack for pups and their humans.

Ingredients

1 (15 oz.) can chick peas
½ tablespoon extra light olive oil
1 tablespoon honey
½ teaspoon ground cinnamon
1/8 teaspoon sea salt

Directions

1. Drain and rinse the chickpeas in a colander. Spread them out between paper towels, pat dry to remove excess water, and let them dry for 30 minutes.
2. In a medium bowl, whisk together the olive oil, cinnamon, and sea salt. Add the chickpeas and coat well.
3. Spread out on a parchment lined baking sheet and bake at 400 degrees for 30 minutes, shaking the pan every 10 minutes, until they are golden and crispy. You'll know when they are done because if you taste one it should be crunchy all the way through. If it's still soft in the middle, continue cooking. If you see that they are getting dark, just lower the temperature in your oven and cook them longer. Keep an eye on them after that so they don't burn which can happen quickly.
4. Remove from the oven, place in a medium bowl and toss with the honey.
5. Place back in the oven and roast for an additional 6 to 7 minutes to caramelize the honey.
6. Cool completely.

I find these won't keep well as they lose their crispness after a day.

Prep Time: 35 minutes	Cook Time: 37 minutes	
Yields: 3 - ½ cups	Calories: 211 each	Calories from fat: 36 each

peanut butter & jelly sandwiches

Ingredients

½ cup natural peanut butter
¼ cup maple syrup
¼ cup almond milk
¼ cup ground flax seed
1 ½ cups buckwheat flour

Peanut butter is a favorite of dogs worldwide. Just ask Kirby who every once in a while can be found in heavenly bliss with his muzzle stuck up inside an almost empty jar so his tongue can reach every last morsel. Dogs love these cookies by themselves but adding a filling just ups the drool factor.

Directions

1. In a large bowl mix together the peanut butter, maple syrup and almond milk. Mix in the flax seed until combined. Then stir in the flour.
2. Roll out about ¼ inch thick and cut out small circles. I use a small biscuit cutter.
3. Place on parchment lined baking sheet and bake at 350° degrees for 12 minutes.
4. Transfer to a baker's rack.
5. Once cooled, add the jelly to half of the cookies and then top with the remaining cookies.

Prep Time: 15 minutes	Cook Time: 12 minutes	
Yields: 46 treats/23 sandwich cookies	Calories: 82/89 each	Calories from fat: 36/37 each

blueberry chia seed jelly

Ingredients

1 cup frozen blueberries
1 tablespoon chia seeds
1 tablespoon honey
1 tablespoon warm water

Directions

1. Blend all of the ingredients in a food processor or blender.
2. Pour the mixture into a mason jar and place in the refrigerator for one hour to let it set.

It will keep up to 2 weeks in the refrigerator or frozen for up to two months.

savory beef bits

I probably make these twice a month. They are perfect for training since they are small and Kirby so loves them. They are greasy so they won't do well in a pocket for obvious reasons. I use them anyway because that boy will do anything and everything I ask not to mention he enthusiastically cooperates for longer training sessions.

Ingredients

- 1 lb. beef stew meat
- 1 tablespoon dried parsley
- 1 tablespoon extra light olive oil

Directions

1. Cut the stew meat into half inch cubes (they will shrink while cooking) and place in a medium size bowl.
2. Add the parsley and olive oil. Using your hands mix until the meat is covered with the oil and parsley.
3. Spread out on foil lined baking sheet.
4. Bake at 350 degrees for 1 hour.
5. Reduce heat to 200 degrees and bake for 2 hours. Let cool.

These will keep in an air tight container in the refrigerator for up to two weeks.
These make great training treats or as a topper for kibble. Kirby drools for these savory bits of beef performing every trick he knows as quickly as he can!

Prep Time: 15 minutes	Cook Time: 3 hours	
Yields: 100+ pieces	Calories: 10 each	Calories from fat: 4 each

frostings for special occasions

These are frostings that harden as they dry.

yogurt frosting

Yields: 1 cup

Ingredients

½ cup plain Greek yogurt
½ cup tapioca starch
2 – 3 teaspoons low fat or 2% milk

Directions

1. Place yogurt and tapioca starch in a small bowl and thoroughly combine.
2. Mix in milk a teaspoon at a time until consistency of frosting.
3. Decorate or dip the dog treats. Place on wax paper and let dry.

Kirby doesn't care for the bland flavor so I sweeten and color it with a very small amount of pureed fruit: strawberries, pineapple, or cherries.

maple frosting

Yields: 1-½ cups

Ingredients

1 cup tapioca starch
¾ cup maple syrup

Directions

1. Place ingredients in a small bowl and thoroughly combine.
2. Chill to thicken before frosting cooled treats.
3. Decorate or dip the dog treats. Place on wax paper and let dry.

carob, peanut butter, or yogurt chips

Yields: ½ cup

Ingredients

½ cup chosen chips
1 tablespoon coconut oil

Directions

1. Place chips and coconut oil in a microwave safe bowl and heat on high for 30 seconds. Stir.
2. Microwave for another 30 seconds. Stir again until smooth.
3. Decorate or simply dip the dog treats. Place on wax paper and let dry.

These are frostings that stay soft.

cream cheese frosting

Yields: 1 cup

Ingredients

1 (4 oz.) package low fat cream cheese
1 tablespoon honey or maple syrup

Directions

1. Let cream cheese come to room temperature.
2. Whip with honey until fluffy.
3. Decorate using a piping bag or spatula.

Make it a pretty color using one drop natural food coloring or ¼ teaspoon dried powder.

pumpkin cream cheese frosting

Yields: 1 cup

Ingredients

1 (4 oz.) package low fat cream cheese
3 teaspoons pure pumpkin

Directions

1. Let cream cheese come to room temperature and blend in the pumpkin until smooth and creamy. You can microwave a few seconds if it's difficult to mix.
2. Decorate using a piping bag or spatula.

bacon cream cheese frosting

Yields: 1 cup

Ingredients

1 (4 oz.} package low fat cream cheese
1 tablespoon maple syrup or honey
¼ cup real bacon bits

Directions

1. Let cream cheese come to room temperature and blend in the maple syrup. You can microwave a few seconds if it's difficult to mix.
2. Stir in the bacon bits.
3. Decorate using a piping bag or spatula.

banana carob frosting

Yields: 1 cup

Ingredients

- 2 medium bananas
- 3 tablespoons whole wheat flour
- 1 tablespoon coconut oil
- 3 tablespoons carob powder
- 2 teaspoons pure vanilla extract
- 1 teaspoon ground cinnamon

Directions

1. Thoroughly mix together all the ingredients and chill in the refrigerator for about twenty minutes.
2. Decorate using a piping bag or spatula.

carob avocado frosting

Yields: 1 cup

Ingredients

- 1 ripe avocado
- ½ cup carob powder
- ½ cup maple syrup
- 2 tablespoons coconut oil

Directions

1. Mix together the ingredients to desired consistency.
2. Refrigerate if it needs to firm up. Add a little water if it is too thick.
3. Decorate using a piping bag or spatula.

mashed potato frosting

Yields: 1 cup

Ingredients

3 peeled and cubed Yukon Gold potatoes
¼ cup low fat or 2% milk
2 tablespoons unsalted butter
2 tablespoons dried parsley

Directions

1. Boil the potatoes, drain and mash.
2. Mix in the remaining ingredients.
3. Decorate using a piping bag or spatula.

I often cheat using 100% real mashed potato flakes to make this.

no bake treats

Even if you don't like to bake, or don't want to bake, we have you covered!

    Christmas Carob Bark...123
    Gummy Paws 124
    Mighty Mutt Balls...127
    PB Pill Pockets 129
    Peanut Butter Cups 131

These liquid treats come in handy when you need to keep your dog hydrated on hot summer days, during heavy exercise, or when they aren't feeling their best. They can be served chilled, slightly warmed, or frozen.

    Bark Beer 132
    Copycat Starbucks Puppucino 133
    Power Punch 135
    Pumpkin Puppucinos 137
    Secret Spinach Smoothies..138
    Strawberry Kefir Milkshake 139

christmas carob bark

The holiday season means it's time to start baking all those scrumptious Christmas cookies and candies. Well now you can make a delicious candy for your dogs! This recipe is fast and easy, and best of all, no baking which means the children can safely make these.

The coconut and carob provide plenty of sweetness so there's no need for any sugars to be added. Adding the peppermint gives them more of a festive taste plus is a great breath freshener but you can leave it out. Instead of almonds you can add peanuts. These are so good I like them!

Ingredients

¾ cup coconut oil
¼ cup carob powder
1 teaspoon peppermint extract
1 snack pack (18) almonds, chopped

Directions

1. Fill a large bowl half way with hot water and then place a medium bowl in the hot water.
2. Add the coconut oil, and once it melts, whisk in the carob powder and peppermint until thoroughly blended. Remove from the hot water and let it sit to thicken up and then whisk again.
3. Mix in the chopped almonds.
4. Spread out the mixture on a baking sheet lined with wax paper.
5. Place in the freezer until hardened.
6. Break into pieces.

You can substitute the same amount of melted carob chips for the carob powder.

Prep Time: 15 minutes	Cook Time: 15 - 20 minutes	
Yields: 30 - 40 small treats	Calories: 46 each	Calories from fat: 43 each

gummy paws

I love to eat Gummy Bears. Kirby wants to eat Gummy Bears but they aren't safe for him since they contain glucose syrup, food coloring, and may contain xylitol known to be toxic for dogs. Now he can have his very own safe Gummy Paws (that he doesn't have to share with us). They're easy to make in a variety of flavors. Once you have the basic recipe you can add finely chopped veggies and fruits. Kirby recommends adding finely chopped meat and bacon bits. Be sure to use only plain, unflavored gelatin such as Knox or Great Lakes not Jell-O Brand which is loaded with artificial coloring and aspartame.

meaty gummy paws

Ingredients

1 cup bone (beef) broth or chicken stock
2 tablespoons or 2 packets gelatin

Directions

1. In a medium saucepan bring the broth to a boil. Remove from heat and let cool for 3 to 4 minutes.
2. Whisk in the gelatin making sure to remove any and all clumps.
3. Allow the mixture to cool and then pour into molds or a jelly roll sheet and cut out shapes.
4. Refrigerate for several hours.

banana lemon gummy paws

Ingredients

2 medium very ripe bananas
¼ cup lemon juice
2 tablespoons or 2 packets gelatin

Directions

1. In a small pot mash the bananas and mix in the lemon juice.
2. Heat over medium low heat until the mixture becomes a loose liquid and then remove from heat.

3. Whisk in the gelatin making sure to remove any and all clumps.
4. Allow the mixture to cool and then pour into molds or pour into a jelly roll sheet and cut out shapes.
5. Refrigerate for several hours.

fruity gummy paws

Ingredients

1 cup fruit juice*
2 tablespoons or 2 packets gelatin

Directions

1. In a medium saucepan bring the juice to a boil. Remove from heat and let cool for 3 to 4 minutes.
2. Whisk in the gelatin making sure to remove any and all clumps.
3. Allow the mixture to cool and then pour into molds or pour into a jelly roll sheet and cut out shapes.
4. Refrigerate for several hours.

*Be sure to use dog friendly juices. DO NOT USE GRAPE JUICE OR CRANBERRY JUICE. Be sure to read the ingredients since many brands use grape juice to sweeten other juice flavors. Juice has a lot of natural sugars so watch the calorie count too.

They can be stored in the refrigerator in an airtight container for up to two weeks.

Mighty Dog Mutt Balls

mighty dog mutt balls

We have a new foster girl who is basically a sack of skin and bones with a horrid bacterial skin infection. The top goal is to get her healthy. She's on medication for the infection, she's eating healthy, homemade foods, and she's getting plenty of exercise. I needed a treat that was healthy and fattening with a flavor she couldn't resist. Last night I had some left over quinoa with lemon and herbs so I gave her a taste test which she happily scarfed down. So quinoa, a superfood, was on the list. I have a pot of bone broth simmering so instead of water I scooped out 2 cups to cook some more quinoa. A good meal in itself but I was going for a treat so I added some peanut butter, healthy but fattening, flaxseed for her coat, and a few seasonings. Natural peanut butter isn't especially sweet so I added some local honey for its' allergy fighting attributes.

Ingredients

- 1 cup quinoa
- 2 cups bone (beef) broth or chicken stock
- ½ cup natural peanut butter
- 2 tablespoons honey
- 2 teaspoons ground flax seed
- ½ teaspoon ground cinnamon
- ½ teaspoon sea salt

Directions

1. In a small pot bring the quinoa and 2 cups bone broth to a boil, cover and simmer for 18 to 20 minutes. Remove from heat. You don't need to drain the quinoa for this recipe.
2. Mix the remaining ingredients in a medium size bowl.
3. Mix in the warm (not hot) quinoa. The warmth will slightly melt the peanut butter and help everything combine.
4. Place in the refrigerator for about 15 minutes to chill and firm up if needed.
5. Use a 1" cookie scooper or teaspoon to make the balls and place onto parchment paper lined baking sheet.
6. Place in the freezer until they are completely firm.

I have received feedback that using store bought broth doesn't always work to bind everything together. I make my own broth which has a lot of gelatin so I recommend adding a packet of unflavored gelatin to the store brand. Warm the broth, whisk in the gelatin, and let sit five minutes before using.

Prep Time: 30 minutes	Cook Time: None	Freeze Time: 1 hour
Yields: 56 – 1" balls	Calories: 29 each	Calories from fat: 13 each

pb pill pockets

Kirby takes two beneficial "treats" on a daily basis - his multivitamin and his hip & joint support - which I now purchase in chewy treat forms. Once a month he takes a heartworm pill and a flea pill which I had to place in Greenies Pill Pockets to trick him into eating them. I tried dipping them in peanut butter but he was smart enough to lick it off and spit out the pill.

There are many dogs that require daily pills for certain illnesses - pills that have to be disguised in order to be taken and not forced or spit out. The Greenies are not only expensive but contain corn products which are considered one of the top three allergens for dogs. Making your own is easy, inexpensive, and healthy.

Ingredients

2 tablespoons brown rice flour
1 tablespoon low fat or 2% milk
1 tablespoon smooth natural peanut butter

Directions

1. Thoroughly mix the ingredients in a small bowl.
2. Form into balls. Optional: Form squares using your fingers.
3. Use the end of a wooden spoon to make small pockets in the center of each.
4. Slide pill into pocket and squeeze dough to cover.

Any fine flour will work: whole wheat, coconut, spelt, barley, etc. Use almond milk or coconut milk if your dog is dairy intolerant. You can also make them in larger quantity using a 2:1:1 ratio. They will last in an air tight zip lock bag for about a week or can be frozen for up to three months letting them thaw out before using.

Dogs should never eat raw bread dough which has yeast causing it to expand in the stomach and can cause alcohol poisoning. Raw flour and sour milk in a warm environment would create yeast over time, however, using fresh milk and storing in a cold environment prevents that from happening.

Prep Time: 15 minutes	Cook Time: None	
Yields: 9 small pockets	Calories: 19 each	Calories from fat: 9 each

Peanut Butter Cups

peanut butter cups

Every time I eat a Reese's Peanut Butter Cup, Kirby puts on his perfected "drool" look - the one where he has the saddest puppy eyes and the tip of his tongue is hanging out. It just slays me every time and I know he knows it! Oh my God how I love this little fluffy boy and to tell him no can be downright heartbreaking but I know chocolate for a dog is poison.

The solution? Creating a Kirby Peanut Butter Cup with carob just for him which is exactly what I did. The little stubby tail going into such a spin as if it could literally lift him off the ground tells me he's happy and the world is right again.

Even though carob looks like, smells like, and has a taste that is similar to chocolate, it does not contain theobromine, the part of chocolate that is toxic to dogs.

Ingredients

1 cup unsweetened carob chips
2 tablespoons coconut oil
2 tablespoons natural peanut butter

Directions

1. Melt the carob chips and coconut oil in a double boiler on the stove stirring until completely smooth. You can also do this in the microwave but I tend to burn it that way.
2. Using a silicone mini mold or mini cupcake liners, fill each one with 1 teaspoon of the carob mixture. Let it sit for about five minutes to harden.
3. Place the peanut butter in a baggie, snip a corner, and squeeze a dab in the center of each carob mound. Press down the peanut butter with your damp finger to flatten it.
4. Cover with 1 teaspoon of the carob mixture.
5. Let them set for about fifteen minutes and voila - dog friendly candy!

You can make them thinner by using "just enough" of the melted carob to cover the bottom of the mold and then "just enough" to cover the peanut butter. These can be kept in an airtight container for a few weeks or in the freezer in a zip-lock bag for several months if they last that long.

Prep Time: 25 minutes	Cook Time: 5 minutes	
Yields: 18 mini cups	Calories: 55 each	Calories from fat: 36 each

bark beer

St. Paddy's Day calls for green so we decided a green beer, for dogs of course, was in order to help celebrate the festive holiday. This is probably the simplest ever with just two ingredients but it does take a little time to "brew". Use chicken stock for a light beer or bone broth for a dark beer.

This nutrient packed "beer" can be poured in a bowl for a cool or warm drink, poured over dry kibble at meal time, or frozen for a hot day.

Ingredients

1 cup chicken stock or bone (beef) broth
2 tablespoons frozen spinach, chopped

Directions

1. Pour the chicken stock into a pint size mason jar.
2. Chop up the spinach and add to the jar. The finer you chop it, the more green color.
3. Let sit in the refrigerator for roughly twenty four hours, shaking it now and then.
4. Strain the spinach and serve.

Frozen spinach provides more green color than fresh spinach leaves. Sometimes I finely chop fresh spinach, cook it in a small pot of water at a rapid boil for about 5 minutes, and then add it to a cup of chicken stock or bone broth without straining it. Either way it's a healthy treat Kirby laps up.

This can be stored in the refrigerator for up to a week and frozen for up to three months.

Prep Time: 24 hours	Cook Time: None	
Yields: 1 cup	Calories: 11	Calories from fat: 5

copycat starbucks puppucino

Ok so I just couldn't resist this one. Kirby finally had his first "Starbucks Puppucino" which is free but in reality cost us almost $14.00 for those fancy cups of joe we couldn't resist. I'm sure he'll have more opportunities but definitely not on a regular basis. It's also rather messy so I was glad we keep doggie wet wipes in the car to clean that sticky muzzle.

Ingredients

- 1 (14 oz) can coconut cream (or 2 cans full-fat coconut milk)
- 2 tablespoons coconut sugar (optional)
- 2 teaspoons vanilla extract

What might you ask is a Starbucks Puppucino? It's a shot of whipped cream served in a little plastic cup free upon request. Kirby loved it, licking that cup cleaner than a dishwasher. I knew this could be replicated at home for a healthier treat without the corn syrup and carrageenan.

Directions

1. Refrigerate the can of coconut cream for 24 hours.
2. Place your metal mixing bowl and beater in the freezer for 5 to 10 minutes to chill.
3. Carefully remove the can of coconut cream from the refrigerator without shaking or tipping it. Remove the top of the can, then use a spoon to carefully spoon out the thick layer of coconut cream that should have separated to the top of the can, and transfer it to your chilled mixing bowl. Stop scooping when you reach the water in the bottom of the can. Save it for another recipe or let your pup drink it.
4. Beat the coconut cream with your whisk attachment on medium speed for 2 to 4 minutes or until the cream becomes light and fluffy and small peaks form. Add in your sweetener and vanilla extract and beat until incorporated.

Don't use "lite" coconut milk and avoid brands with guar gum listed as an ingredient. A can of coconut cream is equivalent to the cream from two cans of coconut milk so only use half the sweetener and vanilla if you are using coconut milk. Other sweeteners to try would be maple syrup or honey. Skip the sweeteners if you're watching calories.

Some brands of coconut milk whip up better than others and even cans of the SAME brand of coconut milk have been known to perform differently. Be advised that if it doesn't work, it may not be you, it may be the brand you're using. I have found that sometimes placing the whipped cream, bowl and beater, in the freezer for about 10 minutes will thicken it up. If all else fails I just pour the mixture into silicon molds and freeze. Kirby is happy either way.

Prep Time: 15 minutes	Cook Time: None	
Yields: 4 – 1/2 cup servings	Calories: 234	Calories from fat: 213

power punch

My original plan was to freeze these as pupsicles but Kirby was hot and thirsty right now. It's always important to keep a dog hydrated so I poured some in a bowl which he greedily lapped up.

These are some of the most potent ingredients for a vibrant and active body. Dogs need hydration especially in the summer months, and while water will do, why not raise the bar both in flavor and health benefits.

Ingredients

- 1 cup decaffeinated green tea
- 1 (13.5 oz.) can lite coconut milk
- 1/2 teaspoon cinnamon
- 2 bananas
- 2 cups frozen or fresh blueberries

Directions

1. Brew one cup of decaffeinated green tea. Caffeine is toxic to dogs so be diligent about this! Set in the refrigerator to cool down. You can use instant green tea as long as there are no added ingredients.
2. Place the remaining ingredients in a blender and puree.
3. Stir in the cooled green tea.

Serve as a drink or freeze in small silicon molds or ice cube trays.

This will keep in the refrigerator for about a week and in the freezer for up to three months.

Prep Time: 10 minutes	Cook Time: 3 minutes	Freeze Time: 2-4 hours
Yields: 10 – 1/2 cup	Calories: 59	Calories from fat: 2

Pumpkin Puppucinos

pumpkin puppucinos

Did you know you can order a puppucino at Starbucks for your dog? It's a shot of whipped cream in a tiny cup. We've gone a little fancier and a little healthier with ours which can also be served as a side dish or mixed with kibble. I use the little plastic bathroom cups which equal 1/4 cup servings. I keep them in the freezer so I can grab a few cups, let them thaw, and warm up in the microwave for about 20 seconds. Your dog is gonna love this treat and you're gonna love how good it is for him!

If pumpkin just can't be found consider substituting with sweet potatoes or squash. To use fresh veggies all you need to do is cook and purée them first. If your dog doesn't like the tang of yogurt, use coconut milk or almond milk.

Ingredients

- 1 (15 oz.) can pure pumpkin
- 1 cup plain Greek yogurt
- 2 teaspoons ground cinnamon
- 1 teaspoon ground ginger
- 1 teaspoon pure vanilla extract
- 2 tablespoons maple syrup or honey

Directions

1. Place all the ingredients except the maple syrup in a medium bowl and whisk until fully blended.
2. Whisk in the maple syrup a tablespoon at a time until you have the desired sweetness. Kirby, my chief taste tester, is quite happy at two tablespoons.

Prep Time: 5 minutes	Cook Time: None	
Yields: 10 – 1/4 cup servings	Calories: 41	Calories from fat: 1

secret spinach smoothies

It's summer. It's hot. Your dog needs hydration. Why not make it nutritional with spinach for powerful antioxidant protection and bone supportive nutrients, green tea for brain function and lower risk of cancer, and local honey for allergies. It has just enough sweetness from the fruit which completely covers the spinach and can be fed as a refreshing drink (add some crushed ice for a slushie) or frozen for quick pick me ups anytime. I love these too but I like to add a little stevia to my glass.

Ingredients

1 cup fresh baby spinach, stems removed
2 bananas
3 kiwis
1 cup decaffeinated green tea
1/2 cup vanilla almond milk
1 tablespoon honey
1 tablespoon chia seeds

Directions

1. Brew the green tea and set aside to cool.
2. Peel and chop the kiwis. Slice the bananas.
3. Place all the ingredients except the chia seeds in a blender or food processor and blend until smooth.
4. Add the chia seeds.
5. Pour into a container with lid and place in the refrigerator for about thirty minutes to let the chia seeds gel.

Serve cold or freeze in individual sized molds or ice cube trays.

Prep Time: 10 minutes	Cook Time: None	
Yields: 3 cups	Calories: 191	Calories from fat: 26

strawberry kefir milkshake

We enjoy homemade milk kefir using different flavors such as maple, cinnamon, and various fruits. Even though it's similar to yogurt, it is a thinner drinkable consistency and is considered much healthier as the probiotics help the body's digestive system. Be sure to start out with small amounts to avoid bloating and gas by giving the body time to adjust. You can purchase readymade kefir at most health food stores and some grocery stores like Whole Foods or you can make it at home like I do. There are also various types of kefir using cow milk, coconut milk, or fruit juices.

I can't think of a healthier way to show my love than with a serving of this delicious pink concoction. I make a batch at a time but if you are using readymade kefir, you can make one cup at a time using the amount of strawberries that satisfies your sweet tooth - this is a drink you can share!

Ingredients

2 cups prepared kefir
2 cups fresh or frozen strawberries

Directions

1. Remove the tops of the strawberries and puree in a food processor or blender.
2. Add the kefir and blend.

Since we drink kefir every day I puree my fruits. When my new batch of kefir is ready, I add some pureed fruit, blend, and pour into mason jars which I store in the refrigerator. The solids and whey will separate but I just shake the jar to reincorporate before drinking.

You can store it in a glass container in the refrigerator for up to 14 days. It can be frozen for up to 3 months since the beneficial probiotics will go dormant until thawed. Leave some headspace for expansion. Place the containers against the walls of the freezer so it freezes as quickly as possible. Let it thaw in the refrigerator at least 24 hours before you plan to use it.

Prep Time: 5 minutes	Cook Time: None	
Yields: 4 – 1/2 cup servings	Calories: 91	Calories from fat: 19

These frosty concoctions are filled with healthy goodness perfect for a hot and humid summer day!

Barkaritas 142
Cinnamon Carob Ice Cream 143
Coconut Ice Cream 145
Decadent PB Pupsicles 147
Did You Say Bacon? Pupsicles 148
Fruity Ice Pups 149
Frosty Freezy Ice Cream 150
Patriotic Pupsicles 151
Pumpkin Pie Pupsicles 152
The Big Bonesicle 153
Yogurt Melts 154

little morsels

For individual servings use silicone molds or small plastic bathroom cups. I buy the 3 oz. plastic bathroom cups at the Dollar Store which come in packages of 50 cups for a buck.

barkaritas

What's better on a hot Saturday afternoon or a sultry night after a long day at Mr. Job? A slushy, cold margarita! My favorite summer drink bar none. Kirby always seems a bit miffed because he can't have one too but, well, there's alcohol in it which is a big no-no for dogs.

Enter the Barkarita! Same slushy coldness but with a flavor a dog can appreciate and no alcohol. A safe, tasty, and healthy way to satisfy a hot, thirsty dog.

Ingredients

frozen chicken stock

Directions

1. Crush two frozen cubes of chicken stock.
2. Place in glass or bowl and serve.

Cheers!

Prep Time: 2 minutes	Cook Time: None	
Yields: 1 serving	Calories: 1	Calories from fat: 1

cinnamon carob ice cream

I love ice cream. So much that I eat a small bowl almost every night of the year. One of my favorite ice creams is Cinnamon Chocolate Ice Cream by Private Selection which is sold exclusively at Kroger. It's only available in the fall months so I stock up when it hits the store.

CHOCOLATE IS TOXIC FOR DOGS so I needed a substitute. Carob looks like, smells like, and tastes similar to chocolate but doesn't contain theobromine, the part of chocolate that is toxic to dogs. I remembered seeing a pin on Pinterest where someone made ice cream with just one ingredient - frozen bananas. A light bulb went off and I knew I could make a dog friendly version so Kirby could indulge in this yummy but unusual concoction of flavors. And truly, it just doesn't get any easier than this!

Ingredients

- 4 medium bananas
- 3 tablespoons carob powder
- 2 teaspoons ground cinnamon

Directions

1. Slice the bananas into disks and freeze. It probably only takes 2 to 4 hours to freeze but I always toss my extra bananas in the freezer and pull out a bag when I need some.
2. Once frozen, mince the bananas in your food processor or chopper. It doesn't look like ice cream yet so don't worry.
3. Move the minced bananas to the mixer and add carob powder and cinnamon. Whip until it is the consistency of a soft serve ice cream.
4. Serve immediately or transfer to a freezer safe container and freeze. For individual servings use small plastic cups and try a bully stick or dog biscuit for the "handle".

You can add any dog friendly flavors to the frozen banana or keep it simple and add nothing. The options are endless!

Prep Time: 10 minutes	Cook Time: 4 hours	
Yields: 8 – 1/2 cup servings	Calories: 111	Calories from fat: 30

coconut ice cream

Kirby loves "human" coconut ice cream. I always end up sharing mine with him since I can't resist those sad brown eyes of his! This is my version of a healthy canine ice cream using coconut milk. I don't have an ice cream maker but you could probably make this with one.

Ingredients

4 large egg yolks
½ cup unsweetened applesauce
2 (13.5 oz.) cans coconut milk
1 tablespoon pure vanilla extract
1 tablespoon blackstrap molasses
1 cup shredded unsweetened coconut

Directions

1. Using a medium size bowl, whisk together the egg yolks and applesauce.
2. Add the coconut milk and whisk until thoroughly blended.
3. Transfer mixture to a pot. (Rinse and dry bowl for later)
4. Cook over medium high heat stirring constantly until mixture somewhat thickens, about 10 minutes. (The egg must be cooked) Remove from heat.
5. Stir in the vanilla, molasses, and shredded coconut.
6. Pour mixture back into the bowl and place in the refrigerator for 2 hours, then in freezer for 30 minutes.
7. Remove bowl from freezer and beat the mixture. Freeze another 30 minutes.
8. Beat mixture again. Freeze another 30 minutes.
9. Beat mixture again. Freeze another 30 minutes. By now it should have a creamy slushy texture and is ready to eat.

You can omit or replace the blackstrap molasses with real maple syrup.

Prep Time: 20 minutes	Cook Time: 4 hours
Yields: 8 – 1/2 cup servings	Calories: 301 Calories from fat: 256

Decadent Pb Pupsicles

decadent pb pupsicles

I had just eaten a bowl of the most scrumptious cinnamon chocolate ice cream ever without sharing even a taste with Kirby. He patiently sat by my side literally drooling as he implored me with those soulful brown eyes of his. It smelled as good as it tasted but we all know what chocolate can do to a dog! Once finished and feeling incredibly guilty I searched my kitchen pantry for something truly doggy decadent in order to make amends.

Ingredients

6 crunchy dog treats
1 cup natural peanut butter
½ cup coconut milk
1 cup plain Greek yogurt
Jerky strips

Directions

1. Place the treats in a baggie and crumble with a rolling pin.
2. Spoon some in the bottom of 9 plastic bathroom cups.
3. Whip peanut butter, coconut milk, yogurt, and remaining cookie crumbles in blender or food processor until a fluffy consistency.
4. Evenly spoon over the cookie crumbles in the cups.
5. Freeze for about twenty minutes then insert jerky strips in centers for the "popsicle sticks".
6. Cover tops with foil and freeze until frozen.
7. The pupsicles should pop out by inverting the cup and giving it a slight squeeze or running cool water under bottoms. Don't use the jerky to pull out.

I do believe I have been forgiven!

Prep Time: 10 minutes	Cook Time: 4 hours	
Yields: 9 – 1/2 cup servings	Calories: 223	Calories from fat: 157
	(doesn't include dog treat or jerky)	

did you say bacon? pupsicles

Kirby and our fosters devour these! I also like bacon, and used to declare these strictly for the dogs! Then along came a really hot day and I ate one. OMG!

Ingredients

1 cup plain Greek yogurt
1 (4 oz.) applesauce
¼ cup low fat or 2% milk
3 tablespoons maple syrup
1 teaspoon cinnamon
1 (3 oz.) bag real bacon bits

Directions

1. In a measuring cup with spout thoroughly whisk together all of the ingredients except the bacon.
2. Whisk in the bacon.
3. Pour the mixture into molds or ice cube trays.
4. Cover with plastic wrap and let freeze for 4 to 6 hours.

Twist to remove. If they won't come out easily hold bottom of molds under cool running water and then twist.

Prep Time: 10 minutes	Cook Time: 4-6 hours	
Yields: 21 – 2" pops	Calories: 79 each	Calories from fat: 22 each

fruity ice pups

Another scorching hot summer day in Mississippi means we need an icy cold treat! Kirby has such a sweet tooth so I love to find healthy treats that can also satisfy his sweet cravings. Whenever I make some juice from concentrate I also make a few cubes for Kirby and our guest dogs. So simple and so healthy!

Ingredients

1 (12 oz.) can concentrate 100% juice (no sugar added)
3 cups cold water

Directions

1. Prepare juice according to directions.
2. Pour into small plastic cups, ice cube trays or silicone molds.
3. Freeze and serve.

These will remain somewhat slushy so if you are making a lot they can be frozen in individual cups for ease of storing and serving. So far Kirby's favorite does seem to be orange juice with pulp. Please remember these are treats, and even though all natural, they have a lot of sugar which can be fattening.

Never use GRAPE JUICE or CRANBERRY JUICE! Read the labels since many brands add grape juice to their fruit juices.

Prep Time: 5 minutes	Cook Time: 2-4 hours	
Yields: 9 – 1/2 cup servings	Calories: 18 each	Calories from fat: 0

frosty freezy ice cream

(Just 2 Ingredients)

Picture this. You get a small bowl of ice cream and snuggle in front of the TV for some "me" time. You check your recorded listings and pick one you've wanted to see when you finally have the time. The show begins, you take a yummy bite savoring the cold sweet flavor, and it's then you notice that furry face staring at you with those sad puppy eyes and just the tiniest bit of tongue hanging out for that pawfect drooling look. You hand him a dry dog friendly treat while you guiltily ignore him to eat the rest of your ice cream.

Now picture this. You get a small bowl of ice cream and snuggle in front of the TV for some "me" time. You check your recorded listings and pick one you've wanted to see when you finally have the time. The show begins, you take a yummy bite savoring the cold sweet flavor as you glance across the room to see your dog happily wagging his tail with his muzzle buried in a bowl of dog friendly ice cream.

Ingredients

2 (13.5 oz.) cans full fat coconut milk (not Lite)
1 cup chopped frozen fruit

Directions

1. Chill the cans of coconut milk overnight which will allow the milk to separate. Some thicken better than others but I usually have success with Thai brand coconut milk.
2. Carefully remove the chilled cans without shaking or tipping them. Open the cans and pour off the watery part of the coconut milk leaving only the milk fat. Scrape out the milk fat from the bottom of the cans into a chilled food processor mixing bowl or high speed blender and blend until thick and creamy.
3. Mix in the chopped fruit.
4. Pour into a 1 quart freezer safe container, cover and freeze for several hours.

This ice cream will eventually freeze into a solid block of ice so you need to put it in a shallow, somewhat long container so you can easily cut it up. Then blend it again which will turn it into a shaved ice consistency. For a creamier texture, place it in a bowl, let it melt a little, and then stir.

Prep Time: 15 minutes	Cook Time: 4 hours	
Yields: 8 – 1/2 cup servings	Calories: 187	Calories from fat: 159

patriotic pupsicles

I love to make red, white and blue treats for Independence Day. It's usually hot hitting the 100's here in Mississippi so something cool and refreshing is always appreciated. These are so easy and healthy for dogs and humans. I enjoy them myself!

Ingredients

- 1 cup fresh strawberries
- 1 cup vanilla Greek yogurt
- 1 cup fresh blueberries
- 1 tablespoon honey

Directions

1. Puree the strawberries and pour even layers in the bottom of 3 inch plastic cups.
2. Set the cups in the freezer for about 10 minutes to let firm. (This will prevent the next layer from bleeding into the previous layer).
3. Next pour a layer of yogurt on top of the set strawberries. You can gently tap the cups on the counter to level the mixture. (If you only have plain yogurt you can add one teaspoon vanilla extract to sweeten it)
4. Again, set the cups in the freezer for 10 minutes to let firm.
5. Next puree the blueberries with the honey to counter the tartness and pour on top of the yogurt. Gently tap on the counter.
6. Cover and freeze for at least six hours. For an added treat push a thin bully stick into the center of each pupsicle after 20 minutes of freezing.

If the pupsicles do not easily release by slightly squeezing or tapping the bottom, hold the bottoms under running cool water for a few seconds to help loosen the pupsicle, then just squeeze out into your hand.

Prep Time: 15 minutes	Cook Time: 4-6 hours	
Yields: 6 – 1/2 cup servings	Calories: 61	Calories from fat: 6

pumpkin pie pupsicles

Here's an easy cool way to give your dog a healthy serving of deliciousness!

Ingredients

1 (15 oz.) can pure pumpkin
Same amount of vanilla Greek yogurt
2 teaspoons ground cinnamon

Directions

1. Pour the pumpkin into a large bowl.
2. Fill the empty can with vanilla Greek yogurt and add to the bowl.
3. Add the cinnamon.
4. Mix well.
5. Spoon into molds or little plastic cups, cover with saran wrap and freeze.

You could also use your ice cream maker, freeze and stir in thirty minute intervals until it has a creamy consistency.

If using plain Greek yogurt add ¼ teaspoon pure vanilla extract.

It's that easy! This has a little twang to it from the yogurt which is ok since Kirby likes yogurt but make sure your dog does.

Prep Time: 5 minutes	Cook Time: 4-6 hours	
Yields: 6 – 1/2 cup servings	Calories: 79	Calories from fat: 15

the big bonesicle

Fostering a large dog requires large treats! The hot humid days of summer require cold treats! Here's a way to satisfy both!

Try making it with bone broth, chicken stock or fruit juice. Instead of dog treats use small pieces of meat, fruit or vegetables. You'll soon discover your pup's favorite flavor combo. Once frozen this can be sliced and saved for individual servings. For smaller dogs like Kirby I freeze it in the silicone muffin tins or plastic bathroom cups.

Ingredients

4 cups bone (beef) broth
Small dog treats

Directions

1. Pour prepared broth into a 9 inch Bundt pan.
2. Add the treats which will sink to the bottom.
3. Place in the freezer until frozen solid.

When ready to serve, place bottom of Bundt pan in warm water for a few seconds. Turn over onto a baking sheet or directly onto the grass. Either way this MUST be served outside to avoid a messy mess!

Prep Time: 5 minutes	Cook Time: 2-4 hours
Yields: 16 servings	Calories: depend on the dog treats used

yogurt melts

Just one tasty, healthy ingredient and you have a handy cold treat for a hot summer day. Super easy too! Just scoop some all natural yogurt into a piping bag and squeeze out drops of goodness. If you don't have a piping bag snip the corner of a baggie or use a plastic squeeze top condiment bottle.

If you use a yogurt with fruit you need to puree it so it won't clog the end of the opening. When choosing the yogurt be sure to read the ingredients - little or no sugar! I like using the Greek yogurts which are a little thicker than regular yogurt.

Ingredients

Low fat plain Greek yogurt

Directions

1. Place the yogurt in a baker's piping bag and pipe drops onto a wax paper lined baking sheet. Don't worry about the drops all matching in size because your dog really won't notice.
2. Place baking sheet in the freezer until yogurt has frozen.
3. Remove to freezer safe plastic container or zip lock bags and store in the freezer.

Just as easy is to blend your own pureed fruit with the yogurt. We have a blueberry bush so I freeze quite a bit when it's producing. Add 1 cup your choice pureed fruit to a 6 oz. tub of plain yogurt.

Let's see, Kirby likes banana, blueberry, cherry, pineapple...

Prep Time: 5 minutes	Cook Time: 20 minutes	
Yields: 50+ melts	Calories: 3 each	Calories from fat: 1 each

fillings for kongs or bones

Dogs are natural problem solvers who enjoy working for their food. The level of difficulty should be adjusted to your dog's level. Too easy and he'll clean his Kong in minutes. Too hard and he'll give up. Easy fillings are loosely packed with small bits of food that can fall out while more difficult fillings are tightly packed with larger pieces that are tricky to get out. Freezing makes it even more difficult. Variety is the spice of life so change it up to keep your dog from getting bored. These are not fillings I created but a compilation of the best ones I have discovered.

Classic Kong Plug small hole with peanut butter. Add canned dog food mixed with kibble. Place a dog treat in the large opening leaving about 1/3 of it sticking out.

Cheesy Elvis Mix together banana, natural peanut butter, real bacon bits, and shredded cheese.

Monster Mash Mix cooked mashed potatoes with crushed dog treats or kibble.

Kongsicle Plug small hole with peanut butter. Fill to the rim with chicken broth. Place a stick or two of beef jerky inside. Freeze.

Banana Yogurt Mix together mashed bananas and plain Greek yogurt.

Peanut Butter Glue Fill 1/3rd full of kibble. Pour in melted peanut butter. Repeat until it's filled. Let the peanut butter cool before serving.

Apple Pie Plug the small hole with a piece of apple. Fill with a mixture of plain Greek yogurt and small chunks of banana and apple.

Crunch 'N Munch: Mix crumbled plain rice cakes with dried fruit and cream cheese.

Pumpkin Pie Mix together plain Greek yogurt, pure pumpkin, and cooked rice.

Breakfast Bone Mix together bananas, unsweetened applesauce, cooked oatmeal, peanut butter, and plain Greek yogurt.

Cheezy Delight Mix shredded cheese with kibble and microwave until the cheese melts. Let cool then pour into the Kong.

Fruitopia Mix applesauce with small chunks of fruit.

dehydrated treats

These treats can be made using a dehydrator or oven. They are easy, healthy and will satisfy your pup's urge to chew and chew and chew.

Bison Jerky 159
Champion Fish Chews 161
Chai Chicken Strips 162
Cherry Fruit Leather 163
Chicken Chompers 165
Doggie Crack aka Pig Ears 167
Love Some Liver Jerky 169
Maple Cinnamon Chicken Jerky 171
My Sweetheart Jerky 172
Oh My Deer Jerky 173
Sweet Potato Chews 174
Turkey Jerky 175
Twice As Good Beef Jerky 177

little morsels

Meat is easiest to slice if it's cold or frozen. I use kitchen shears to cut frozen chicken and fish into strips.

Line your dehydrator trays and baking sheets with silpat, parchment paper, wax paper, or foil to prevent sticking. Good quality plastic wrap can be used in the dehydrator.

There are two ways to make your jerky – in the oven at the lowest setting turning over as one side is done, or in a dehydrator which, with all the commercial jerky recalls of late, is a great investment.

Store your completely cooled jerky in an air tight container for up to three weeks avoiding the refrigerator which will cause moisture and mold. You can freeze jerky for up to six months wrapped in aluminum foil and placed in zip lock bags.

bison jerky

Here's an easy recipe for jerky using only one ingredient. Ground bison, commonly known as buffalo, is a nutrient dense meat. It's expensive at roughly $8.00 per pound but well worth a splurge now and then. However, any ground meat will delight your pups.

Ingredients

1 lb. ground bison

Directions for dehydrator

1. Line the tray with plastic wrap or paper.
2. Using your fingers press the meat mixture into a very thin layer on the tray.
3. Dehydrate until the meat has firmed up which will take about 2 hours.
4. Remove the meat from the plastic wrap, cut into strips, and place back on the tray least cooked side up.
5. Continue dehydrating until the meat is completely dry.

Directions for oven

1. Puree the meat in a food processor.
2. Using a spatula or your hands, spread out the meat on a lined baking sheet.
3. Bake at 200 degrees for 2 hours leaving the oven door slightly ajar to let moisture escape.
4. Remove from the oven and slice into strips or bite size pieces. You can use a knife but a pizza cutter is amazingly quick and easy.
5. Place pieces, flipped over, back on baking sheet and return to the oven.
6. Continue baking for 3 more hours.
7. Turn off the oven and leave in until the pieces are dry and leathery.

Check often and use a paper towel to dab the tops to remove the juices as the jerky cooks. You can discard the paper once the jerky is not dripping juices. It's less messy to partially bake it in the oven, then transfer to the dehydrator.

Prep Time: 10 minutes	Cook Time: 3-4 hours	
Yields: 30 small strips	Calories: 36 each	Calories from fat: 21 each

Champion Fish Chews

champion fish chews

Kirby absolutely adores his fish jerky so I vary it up with different seasonings tailored to his preferences. If your dog has allergies to chicken then this is a healthy, low fat alternative. I've been making these a long time but when Kirby won his first fetch game at the Annual Humane Society Pool Party I officially named them Champion Fish Chews in his honor.

Ingredients

1 lb. tilapia
2 tablespoons extra light olive oil
1 teaspoon lemon juice
1 teaspoon dill seed
1 teaspoon dried parsley

Directions

1. Make sure the fish is deboned then cut in half long ways with kitchen shears while still frozen.
2. Thaw out by placing them in one layer on a baking sheet. Any fish will do but Kirby's fave is tilapia.
3. Place the thawed fish in a large bowl and add the remaining ingredients.
4. Coat the pieces well and place in a single layer on a foil lined baking sheet. Pour the remaining juices over the fish.
5. Bake at 200 degrees for one hour.
6. The fish is cooked when it easily flakes so go ahead and feed a small meal to your pups.
7. Continue to bake the fish in the oven on low heat for several hours (turning over once) until dried or move the fish to your dehydrator. Be sure to line with paper for easy cleanup. When the pieces are somewhat dry, remove the paper for quicker drying.

Kirby loves Tilapia but any fish will work. Let the baking sheet cool and then let the dogs lick up all those yummy juices before throwing the foil away.

Prep Time: 5 minutes	Cook Time: 8-10 hours	
Yields: 16 large pieces	Calories: 39 each	Calories from fat: 18 each

chai chicken strips

Tea spiced with ginger, cinnamon and anise is often referred to as chai tea. Replace the tea with chicken and, viola, a tasty, healthy snack your pup will devour!

Everyone knows cats love catnip but did you know that dogs can react to anise in the same way? Like cats, some dogs are affected more than others but any dog will enjoy the licorice scent and flavor of this herb.

Ingredients

   3 lbs. boneless, skinless chicken breasts
   2 tablespoons coconut oil
   1 teaspoon ground ginger
   1 teaspoon ground cinnamon
   1 teaspoon anise oil or ground anise powder

Directions for dehydrator

1. Either thinly slice or pound out the breasts with a rolling pin. Cut into the size strips you want with kitchen shears remembering they will shrink as they cook.
2. Place in a medium size bowl and add the coconut oil. If it is solidified just use the warmth of your hands to melt it and then rub over the chicken.
3. Add the seasonings. Again, using your hands, thoroughly mix until certain they have been thoroughly distributed.
4. Place in your dehydrator and cook on high for 8 to 10 hours. Turn the chicken pieces over when the top side has dried.

Directions for oven

1. Place the prepared pieces of chicken on a lined baking sheet.
2. Bake at 200 degrees for 2 hours leaving the oven door slightly ajar to let moisture escape.
3. Remove from the oven and flip pieces over.
4. Return to the oven and continue baking until the pieces are dry.

Prep Time: 10 minutes	Cook Time: 8-10 hours	
Yields: 40+ strips	Calories: 71 each	Calories from fat: 29 each

cherry fruit leather

Fruit leathers, or roll ups, can be healthy, satisfying bites of sweetness or tartness with a unique chewy texture. Fresh fruit has to be heated to kill off potential pathogens before using it so you can skip that step since canned fruit has already been heated. Choose fruit packed in water only. Try different fruits, veggies, and seasonings to discover your dog's fave flavors keeping in mind that flavors and sweetness intensify after drying so less is more. For light colored fruits, add a teaspoon of lemon juice to prevent browning. If it's too thick to pour just add a little juice from the can or water.

Ingredients

- 1 (14.5 oz.) can red tart cherries
- 1 large banana
- 1 teaspoon pure vanilla extract
- 1 tablespoon honey

Directions for dehydrator

1. Drain the cherries in a colander and puree all of the ingredients in a blender or food processor.
2. Pour the mixture in the center of each lined tray and spread with a spatula until it is between 1/4 and 1/8 inch thick spreading evenly so all areas dry in the same amount of time.
3. Dehydrate until it looks translucent, is only slightly sticky to the touch, and peels easily away from the plastic wrap.

Directions for oven

1. Prepare as above using a lined baking sheet.
2. Bake at the lowest temperature your oven has for roughly 4 hours. It's ready when it looks translucent and the center is only slightly sticky to the touch.

Once done transfer to a sheet of parchment paper while it's still warm. Place another sheet of parchment paper on top. Use kitchen shears to cut into strips, roll, and tie with twine or use a piece of tape.

Plastic wrap or silicone baking sheets work best since the fruit mixture will stick to foil and parchment paper which you can still use as long you spray it with a non-stick spray or brush it with vegetable oil first

The edges will cook faster than the center so if they look like they're getting crispy just brush them with a little water or juice or cut them off and discard. If you over bake the entire pan, you can brush with a little water until it's pliable again

Prep Time: 5 minutes	Cook Time: 4 hours	
Yields: 16 strips	Calories: 21 each	Calories from fat: 0 each

chicken chompers

I make these every month. The dangerous recalls, the inexpensive cost of chicken, the fact most dogs enjoy a good chew. There are plenty of reasons to make this your go to recipe.

Ingredients

- 1 (3 lb.) bag boneless, skinless chicken breasts
- 2 tablespoons dried rosemary
- 2 tablespoons dried parsley

Directions for dehydrator

1. Thaw chicken then rinse well under cool water.
2. Cut away all of the fat. Using kitchen shears, cut the breasts in half long ways.
3. Lay the pieces on wax paper and lightly pound with a meat tenderizer. You can use a rolling pin but I like how the meat tenderizer pierces the meat allowing the seasonings to seep into the meat while drying.
4. Place the pieces in a medium size bowl and add the seasonings. Over time I have learned these are Kirby's favorite combo for chicken but you can use any combination of dog safe herbs your dog may prefer.
5. Using your hands, toss the chicken to thoroughly coat with the seasonings.
6. Place the chicken pieces in the dehydrator on paper to avoid sticking.
7. Let dry until the top side has dried to the touch, roughly an hour.
8. Turn pieces over and discard the paper. Let them dehydrate until thoroughly dried which will take several hours.

Directions for oven

1. Place the prepared pieces of chicken on a lined baking sheet.
2. Bake at 200 degrees for 2 hours leaving the oven door slightly ajar to let moisture escape.
3. Remove from the oven and flip pieces over.
4. Return to the oven and continue baking until the pieces are dry.

Warning: You will have a captive audience underfoot until the first one is tested! Kirby always seems to know the difference when I'm making human foods or his meals and treats.

Prep Time: 15 minutes	Cook Time: 4-6 hours	
Yields: 18 pieces	Calories: 145 each	Calories from fat: 51 each

Doggie Crack Aka Pig Ears

doggie crack aka pig ears

Kirby so loves chomping on those pig ears. In fact whenever I gave him a pig ear or snout he would work on it until the very last bite was gone. Nothing could distract him from this task! About a year ago manufactured pig ears for dogs began to be recalled mostly due to salmonella bacteria. I couldn't keep up with which ones were recalled and which ones were deemed safe so I just stopped buying them altogether. Now I can give him one of his favorite chews knowing its safe!

Ingredients

    4 large pig ears
    1 tablespoon sea salt
    ½ teaspoon garlic powder
    2 tablespoons ham flavored bouillon

Directions

1. First you need to remove any hairs on the ears. I purchase mine from a local Asian Market so that's already done. You can shave off the hairs with a razor or burn them off with a kitchen torch or butane lighter.
2. Next you need to remove any bacteria or impurities from the surface of the ears prior to cooking. Fill a large stock pot three-fourths full of cold water. Place the pig ears into the pot of water and bring to a boil. Immediately remove the pot from the burner. Remove the pig ears to a colander and rinse under cool running water.
3. Rinse out the pot and refill with cold tap water until it is three-fourths full. Add the seasonings to the water. Place the pig ears back into the pot and allow it to come to another boil. Turn down the heat to a low simmer for about fifteen to twenty minutes to allow the ears to soak up the flavors.
4. Remove the ears and dry on paper towels. Depending on the size of your dog you may now want to cut the ears into smaller strips with kitchen shears.
5. Place the pig ears in a single layer on a foil covered baking sheet.
6. Spray or brush both sides of each ear with olive oil or vegetable oil.
7. Bake at 200 degrees for up to five hours until the ears are a crispy brown color and very hard to bend which means most of the moisture has been removed. You could also use your dehydrator at this point.

If you want flat pig ears like the store bought, just slice through the curling part with kitchen shears while they are baking. They are a little bit oily when done so just wipe them with a paper towel.

This does take a long time but is so worth it! I bet Kirby never thought he would taste another yummy pig ear in his lifetime, hence the name "Doggie Crack".

Also, remember pig ears next time someone lights up the smoker!

WARNINGS!

Pork, like chicken, can produce salmonella so be sure to clean everything it touches. Be very careful where you purchase your pig ears! You could probably purchase in bulk from a slaughterhouse but then you wouldn't really know how fresh they are. Foods sold for human consumption in the U.S. are regulated so to be safe I would only purchase from a local market.

Pig ears, unlike rawhide, are considered to be slowly digestible. That said you should still monitor your dog every time he or she is eating any chew. If the dog doesn't chew it enough they can swallow large pieces which could cause an obstruction in their esophagus or stomach. If you see your dog isn't chewing enough then try cutting the strips into smaller pieces.

Pig ears have a very high fat content so I recommend no more than one a week and never give any to a dog suffering from pancreatis.

Pig ears can be stored in a paper bag or wrapped in paper for up to six months and in the freezer indefinitely. Don't use plastic containers which cause moisture retention making the chews soft and moldy.

Prep Time: 60 minutes	Cook Time: 5 hours	
Yields: 12 strips	Calories: 64 each	Calories from fat: 38

love some liver jerky

This is so easy to make in the dehydrator. The first time I made them, I placed them on a plate, gave Kirby one strip, and became busy doing other things. A few hours later I went into the kitchen intent on giving Kirby one more piece and refrigerating the rest. What rest? Much to Kirby's dismay, one of our cats, Chelsea, very much likes liver! The plate was completely empty. Not even a morsel for Kirby to savor.

I have to confess I usually make liver jerky on days I can leave the back door open, and once done, spray a few shots of an air freshener. Kirby adores the aroma, the rest of us not so much. I purchase 1 lb. calf liver which comes in 4 individual slices I then cut into strips

Ingredients

½ lb. calf liver

Directions for dehydrator

1. Thinly slice while it's still frozen. It will thaw very quickly.
2. Dehydrate on lined dehydrator trays.
3. Remove the paper once the tops are dry and place back on the tray cooked side up.
4. Continue dehydrating until strips are dry.

Directions for oven

1. Bake on a lined baking sheet at 200 degrees leaving the oven door slightly ajar to let moisture escape.
2. Remove from the oven when top side is dry and flip pieces over.
3. Return to the oven and continue baking until the pieces are dry.

When working with liver, be sure you clean as you go! Liver dries very quickly and can become extremely difficult to remove so I am careful to completely rinse each item as I use it.

It's a good idea to monitor how much pure liver your dog eats. Small amounts or less than three servings a week are very good for your dog. However, large amounts can cause vitamin A toxicity which can lead to bone problems, weight loss, and anorexia. Never feed your dog liver if he is taking vitamin A supplements.

Prep Time: 5 minutes	Cook Time: 4-8 hours	
Yields: 14 strips	Calories: 28 each	Calories from fat: 7 each

Maple Cinnamon Chicken Jerky

maple cinnamon chicken jerky

Kirby "the carnivore" loves his meaty jerky whether it be chicken, beef, venison, or fish. I'm always testing new flavor combinations trying to utilize ingredients that are not only tasty but provide healthy benefits for his body. Once I clean the chicken breasts removing all the fat and silvery membrane I like to slice them horizontally so I have long thin slices. They will shrink a lot as they dehydrate.

Cutting with the grain creates chewy, fibrous strips while cutting against the grain creates more tender, leathery strips. If your dog is a good chewer then cut with the grain. If your dog chews quickly or not at all, then cut against the grain. If you don't have a dehydrator you can still make these in the oven at the lowest temperature flipping regularly.

Ingredients

- 3 lbs. boneless, skinless chicken breasts
- 3 tablespoons maple syrup
- 1 teaspoon ground cinnamon

Directions for dehydrator

1. Slice the chicken breasts lengthwise which is easiest to do while still frozen.
2. Add the maple syrup and cinnamon to a small jar and shake until combined.
3. Place the chicken slices in a sealable container. Pour the maple syrup and cinnamon marinade over the chicken, cover and turn over several times to completely cover the chicken.
4. Refrigerate for about thirty minutes, turning the container over to help disburse the marinade.
5. Place the chicken pieces on wax or parchment paper.
6. Dehydrate for 8 to 10 hours turning over once the bottom side is dried. You can now discard the paper.
7. Remove when completely dried.

Directions for oven

1. Place the prepared pieces of chicken on a lined baking sheet.
2. Bake at 200 degrees for 2 hours leaving the oven door slightly ajar to let moisture escape.
3. Remove from the oven and flip pieces over.
4. Return to the oven and continue baking until the pieces are dry.

Prep Time: 40 minutes	Cook Time: 8-10 hours	
Yields: 22 large slices	Calories: 125 each	Calories from fat: 41 each

my sweetheart jerky

Known as the poor man's steak, beef hearts are a healthy choice when it comes to your dog. It's a dense muscle with a high nutrient content and protein. There is a little more work involved than just slicing and dehydrating but at less than $3 for a beef heart this is the cheapest jerky you'll ever make.

I've heard there are some places you can purchase beef hearts already prepared. That's not the case for me. So to prepare the beef heart cut away the tough, fatty top of the heart containing valves and tendons. Next soak it in cold, salted water for 1 to 2 hours so that excess blood will be rinsed away. You can add 1 cup of apple cider vinegar for more tender meat and to remove the strong odor. Next carefully cut away the membrane and fat from the meat getting as close as possible.

Ingredients

   1 beef heart
   2 (6 oz. cans) pine-orange-banana juice
   1 tablespoon apple cider vinegar
   ½ teaspoon garlic powder
   ¼ teaspoon cayenne pepper
   ¼ teaspoon ground ginger

Directions for dehydrator

1. Cut the meat into ¼ inch thick strips and place in a sealable container.
2. Mix together the remaining ingredients and microwave for one minute to warm up.
3. Pour the marinade over the beef heart, close lid, and turn over several times to coat all the pieces.
4. Place in the refrigerator overnight. Turn container over now and then to let the marinade seep into every piece.
5. Drain the excess marinade. Place the strips on lined dehydrator trays and dehydrate for 6 to 8 hours until the jerky is dry but still flexible. Flip pieces over as they become dry on one side.

Directions for oven

1. Place the prepared jerky on a lined baking sheet.
2. Bake at 200 degrees for 2 hours leaving the oven door slightly ajar to let moisture escape.
3. Remove from the oven and flip pieces over.
4. Return to the oven and continue baking until the pieces are dry.

Prep Time: 2 hours	Cook Time: 6-8 hours	
Yields: 40 strips	Calories: 47 each	Calories from fat: 3 each

oh my deer jerky

Venison is an excellent source of protein with practically no fat but you have to know a hunter. Luckily I have a friend who has a friend who is a hunter. These smell so good you'll want to chew on a few yourself!

Ingredients

- 1 lb. ground venison
- 1 teaspoon cayenne pepper
- 2 teaspoons garlic powder

Directions for dehydrator

1. Use your hands to thoroughly mix the ingredients.
2. Cover and refrigerate for at least 2 hours or overnight.
3. Using your fingers press the meat mixture into a very thin layer on the lined tray.
4. Dehydrate until the meat has firmed up which will take about 2 hours.
5. Remove the meat from the plastic wrap, cut into strips, and place back on the tray, least cooked side up so it won't stick to the tray.
6. Continue dehydrating until the meat is completely dry.

Directions for oven

1. Use your hands to thoroughly mix the ingredients.
2. Cover and refrigerate for at least 2 hours or overnight.
3. Roll out the meat to an even thickness (about 1/8") between two sheets of wax paper.
4. Place in the freezer until frozen.
5. Remove and cut into strips. Remember they will shrink while cooking.
6. Line the baking sheet with foil and lightly spray with olive oil.
7. Remove the top piece of wax paper, lay the jerky on the baking sheet, and then remove the second piece of paper.
8. Bake at the lowest temperature your oven will go (mine is 170 degrees) for 3 to 4 hours flipping over when one side is dry.

Prep Time: 2 hours	Cook Time: up to 10 hours	
Yields: 30 small strips	Calories: 29 each	Calories from fat: 11 each

sweet potato chews

Another great fall root vegetable is the sweet potato. They are a powerhouse of nutrition, bursting with beta carotene (vitamin A), high in vitamin C, a good source of fiber, fat-free and cholesterol-free. In fact, the sweet potato has taken top honors in two surveys of the nutritional benefits of vegetables. When eaten with the skin, it has more fiber than oatmeal. One medium sweet potato, baked with the skin, has about four times the recommended daily allowance (RDA) of vitamin A and almost half the recommendation for vitamin C.

These chews are super easy to make.

Ingredients

1 small sweet potato
2 tablespoons blackstrap molasses

Directions for dehydrator

1. Wash the sweet potato and pat dry.
2. Slice as thin as possible. A Mandolin makes this easy.
3. Place ingredients in zip-lock bag and mix well until all the slices are coated. Place on lined dehydrator trays.
4. Dehydrate until the chews have the desired texture and dryness you want.

Directions for oven

1. Place the prepared pieces on a lined baking sheet.
2. Bake at 200 degrees for 2 hours leaving the oven door slightly ajar to let moisture escape.
3. Remove from the oven and flip pieces over.
4. Return to the oven and continue baking until dry.

There are so many liquid flavors you can try... honey, chicken stock, bone broth, even carob molasses. Kirby's favorite? Given a choice he goes for the blackstrap molasses every time.

I would suggest keeping them in an air tight container in the refrigerator unless you have completely dried yours. Watch for any mold and throw out at the first sign.

Prep Time: 10 minutes	Cook Time: 2-4 hours	
Yields: 20 slices	Calories: 11 each	Calories from fat: 0

turkey jerky

Who says turkey is just for Thanksgiving when you have this healthy, tasty, easy recipe!

Ingredients

1 lb. ground turkey
1 tablespoon extra light olive oil

Directions for dehydrator

1. Line the tray with plastic wrap or paper.
2. Using your fingers press the meat mixture into a very thin layer on the tray.
3. Dehydrate until the meat has firmed up which will take about 2 hours.
4. Remove the meat, cut into strips, and place back on the tray, cooked side down.
5. Continue dehydrating until the meat is completely dry.

Directions for oven

1. Puree the meat with the olive oil in a food processor.
2. Using a spatula, spread it out on a lined baking sheet.
3. Bake at 200 degrees for 2 hours leaving the oven door slightly ajar to let moisture escape.
4. Remove from the oven, wipe up grease, and flip over. Continue baking for 3 more hours.
5. Remove and slice into strips or bite size pieces with a knife or pizza cutter.
6. Place the strips back on the baking sheet and return to the oven.
7. Continue cooking for several more hours until the pieces are dry and leathery.

Check often and use a paper towel to dab the tops to remove the juices as the jerky cooks. You can discard the paper once the jerky is not dripping juices. It's less messy to partially cook in the oven, then transfer to the dehydrator.

I received an email from a fan asking about adding banana to this recipe since her dog loves an expensive Banana Turkey treat she buys on a regular basis. Absolutely! Mash and mix in one ripened banana in place of the olive oil.

Prep Time: 10 minutes	Cook Time: 8 hours	
Yields: 30 small strips	Calories: 34 each	Calories from fat: 19 each

Twice As Good Beef Jerky

twice as good beef jerky

Kirby loves some jerky. To make it stretch further I sometimes combine ground beef with calf liver. It's easy and cheaper on the budget. Often times I like to add a few herbs for their flavor and benefit. Kirby likes the flavor rosemary imparts which is a good thing since it's a great preservative. Calf liver is preferred over beef liver because fewer toxins have filtered through a younger animal. Liver in large amounts can cause Vitamin A toxicity so feed sparingly.

Remember when working with liver to rinse utensils immediately after use or you'll be scrubbing and scrubbing to get that dried stuff off.

Ingredients

1 lb. ground beef
1 cup calf liver

Directions for dehydrator

1. Puree the calf liver and then mix it in with the ground beef.
2. This is messy so line your dehydrator with paper for easy cleanup.
3. Scoop the meat into a Jerky gun or zip lock bag and snip a corner so you can squeeze out the meat mixture. Squeeze out 2 inch long strips and place on the waxed paper. Press down to flatten.
4. Dehydrate for about 3 to 4 hours. At this point it really looks like dog poo but it does look better when done.
5. Remove the wax paper and turn over the meat to dry out the other side. Dehydrate another 3 to 4 hours until the meat is dry and crunchy.

Directions for oven

1. Place the prepared meat on a lined baking sheet.
2. Bake at 200 degrees for 2 hours leaving the oven door slightly ajar to let moisture escape.
3. Remove from the oven and slice into strips.
4. Return to the oven cooked side down and continue baking until the pieces are dry.

Squeezing out the strips takes some muscle so you may want to spoon out teaspoonfuls and flatten. The fatter the strips, the longer to dehydrate.

Prep Time: 20 minutes	Cook Time: 7+ hours	
Yields: 53 to 55 2" strips	Calories: 23 each	Calories from fat: 6 each

meals

The same dry kibble day after day? I think not when you have so many wholesome, fresh ingredients to choose from. It does require a little time but a batch can make many nourishing meals with the added bonus of knowing exactly what your dog is eating. Remember a dog's diet requires 70 percent moisture so every time he eats dry kibble his body has to provide sufficient moisture to reconstitute the food in the digestive tract which stresses multiple organs, especially the kidneys.

If feeding 50 percent or more homemade meals be sure to supplement with a daily pet multi-vitamin and use the ground egg shell measurements included in each recipe. If your dog eats mostly commercial food then omit the ground egg shell.

Arroz Con Pollo	181
Beefy Kale Pasta	183
Breakfast Porridge	185
Chazuke	186
Chicken Barley Soup	187
Chicken Gizzard Casserole	188
Chicken Gumbo	189
Cottage cheese Muttins	191
Greek Lamb Patties	193
Hamburger Helper Canine Style	195
Little Italy Meatballs	197
Meaty Muffins	198
Muttloaf	199
Sheperd's Pie	201
Southwestern Chicken Chili	202
The Carnivore's Cake	203
Turkey Burgers	204
Viva La Venison	205

little morsels

¼ teaspoon ground egg shell is recommended per pound of meat for calcium for dogs who eat mostly homemade. I have included that requirement in each recipe. This is not necessary if your dog eats mostly commercial dog food.

Vegetables are harder for a dog to digest so they should be finely chopped or shredded to pre-digest allowing for proper release and absorption of nutrients.

Choose natural baby food containing only water.

Kirby is accustomed to a wide variety of meals. However, some dogs may get upset tummies so it's helpful to switch from commercial foods to homemade gradually. A few tablespoons of pure pumpkin can do wonders for diarrhea or constipation.

I make these meals in batches and then freeze for future meals. Once they are thawed I warm them in the microwave for about 20 seconds. Meals should be served at room temperature or slightly warmed in the microwave to avoid burning the dog's mouth.

I use fresh herbs from my garden whenever possible but I understand many may not have that luxury. For convenience I have listed the dry/ground herb ingredient amounts in the recipes with a conversion chart for using fresh herbs under The pantry.

Use parchment paper muffin cups when making the meat muffins for easy cleanup.

Unless otherwise noted, these meals will keep in the refrigerator for up to five days and up to three months in the freezer.

arroz con pollo

Arroz Con Pollo is Spanish for "rice with chicken". The classic recipe calls for white rice, roma tomatoes, and several spices. This is my standard super easy "Kirby" version which is good for when your dog may be ailing. It's one of my go-to recipes for new fosters to help strengthen their weak immune systems and start adjusting their bodies to good nutrition.

Sometimes I boil chicken breasts but this recipe is a great way to use leftover chicken - baked, grilled, or roasted. Just make sure there weren't a lot of seasonings used. Also, you can add more stock to the final dish if you want, or need, more liquid.

Ingredients

   2 to 3 chicken breasts
   2 cups cooked brown rice
   2 ½ cups chicken stock
   2 (3.5 oz.) jars natural sweet potato baby food
   2 teaspoons dried parsley
   ¼ teaspoon ground egg shell

Directions

1. Boil the chicken breasts. Discard the skin and bones. Shred the meat. If you don't have any chicken stock use the water you boiled the chicken in.
2. Cook the rice using a ratio of 2 1/2 cups chicken stock to 1 cup rice so the rice gets to the point of mush since a dog's body has a harder time digesting grains.
3. Thoroughly mix together. Let cool and serve.

Prep Time: 10 minutes	Cook Time: 30 minutes	
Yields: 8 – 1/2 cup servings	Calories: 246	Calories from fat: 23

beefy kale pasta

This simple meal is packed with flavor Kirby loves and nutrients he needs. If you can't find any kale, spinach is a good substitute. Cayenne pepper gives a little kick Kirby seems to really like.

Ingredients

- 1 lb. ground beef
- 3 cups chopped kale
- 2 small chopped red peppers
- ¼ teaspoon sea salt
- ½ teaspoon cayenne pepper
- 1 teaspoon garlic powder
- ¼ teaspoon ground egg shell
- 2 cups cooked pasta

Directions:

1. In a large skillet cook the ground beef, peppers and kale over medium heat until the meat is fully cooked.
2. Stir in the seasonings and let simmer on low for five minutes.
3. Meanwhile cook the pasta to the point of being mushy. Drain and rinse, rinse, and rinse again to remove as much of the starch as possible. Add the pasta to the skillet and thoroughly mix.
4. Let cool and serve.

I like to use the smallest pasta I can find to help with digestion while providing needed carbohydrates.

Prep Time: 10 minutes	Cook Time: 30 minutes	
Yields: 8 – 1 cup servings	Calories: 283	Calories from fat: 39

Breakfast porridge

breakfast porridge

Want something healthy and super easy for those days you have a long excursion planned requiring lots of energy from your dog? This make ahead breakfast is chock full of wholesome deliciousness dogs will devour.

I believe dogs are carnivores by nature so I only prepare this once in a while since there is no meat.

Ingredients

- 1 cup old fashioned oats
- ½ cup vanilla almond milk
- ½ teaspoon ground cinnamon
- ½ cup pure pumpkin
- 2 tablespoons blackstrap molasses
- ½ cup dried pineapple

Directions

1. Mix together all the ingredients in a container with lid.
2. Place in the refrigerator overnight.
3. In the morning stir and serve. Sometimes I throw in some bacon bits.

Kirby likes his with almond milk but feel free to use low fat or 2% milk, coconut milk, or rice milk. He also likes it heated for about 15 seconds in the microwave, actually he likes all of his meals warmed.

Chopped fresh fruit can be added in the morning. If using dried fruit then do add it the night before to give it time to absorb moisture to plump up.

This will not freeze well.

Prep Time: 10 minutes	Cook Time: 15 seconds	
Yields: 4 servings	Calories: 218	Calories from fat: 27

chazuke

Chazuke is a light rice dish popular in Japan. As "chai" means tea in Japanese, hot green tea is simply poured over steamed rice and various toppings. Leftover steamed rice is often used for this dish. This is my dog friendly version which can easily be shared with the humans. Kirby loves fish but you can use any shredded cooked meat such as chicken or turkey.

Green tea is a calming tea rich in anti-oxidants and has been found to be helpful in fighting some cancers. You can easily shred a few small carrots in place of the baby food. Dried kelp can be found at any Asian market or ordered online.

Ingredients

1 cup parboiled rice
3 decaffeinated green tea bags
¼ teaspoon sea salt
¼ teaspoon ginger
1 (14.7 oz.) can drained and deboned salmon
1 (4 oz.) jar natural carrot baby food
¼ teaspoon ground egg shell
2 strips Kombu kelp (optional)

Directions

1. Steep three cups of tea. Remember to choose decaffeinated as caffeine is toxic for dogs.
2. Cook the rice according to package directions but substitute the water with two cups of the brewed green tea. Add the ginger and sea salt before bringing the rice to a boil.
3. Meanwhile cook the kelp by bringing a small pot of water to a boil and then simmering for 20 minutes. Drain and chop into small pieces.
4. Pour the cooked rice into a large bowl and stir in the last cup of green tea, salmon, baby food, and optional kelp until thoroughly mixed.

Prep Time: 35 minutes	Cook Time: 37 minutes	
Yields: 6 – 1 cup servings	Calories: 210	Calories from fat: 40

chicken barley soup

Soup is good any time of the year since it can be eaten cold or warmed up. Soup contains water which is a great benefit to a dog's digestive system for new cell formation, detoxification, removal of waste, temperature regulation, nutrient absorption and digestion. There's a reason people say soup is good for the soul... and cold days... and sick ones... and, well you get the idea.

Barley, which adds a delicious nutty flavor, can be omitted if you prefer grain free. If so, then reduce the amount of water by two cups.

Ingredients

- 4 chicken breasts
- 8 cups water
- 1 tablespoon extra light olive oil
- ¼ teaspoon garlic powder
- ½ teaspoon sea salt
- ¼ teaspoon cayenne pepper
- ½ teaspoon basil
- 2 tablespoons dried parsley
- ¼ teaspoon ground egg shell
- 2 chopped small green peppers
- 1 cup chopped celery
- 2 cups chopped carrots
- 1 cup soaked barley

Directions

1. Place the chicken breasts in a Dutch oven or stockpot. Add the water and olive oil. Cook over medium to medium high heat until the chicken is cooked. Remove the chicken from the pot and let cool. Discard any bones and skin, then shred or dice into small pieces.
2. Lower the heat to a simmer. Add the seasonings, veggies, and drained barley to the pot. Cover and let simmer for about 45 minutes until the veggies are really tender and the barley is well cooked.
3. Add the chicken back to the pot.
4. Let cool and serve.

Prep Time: 20 minutes	Cook Time: 65 minutes	
Yields: 12 –1 cup servings	Calories: 169	Calories from fat: 47

chicken gizzard casserole

This was a great success! Kirby and our current foster ~~Odie~~ Dobby, licked their bowls clean! The majority of Kirby's meals include brown rice as a grain so barley is a nice change for him. Easy, healthy, tasty - what more can a pet parent ask for?

Ingredients

1 ½ lbs. boiled and chopped chicken gizzards
2 cups chopped frozen or fresh spinach
1 (15 oz.) can pure pumpkin
1 cup dried cranberries
1 tablespoon safflower oil
3 cups barley
¼ teaspoon ground egg shell

Directions

1. Cook the barley following directions on the box. Kirby doesn't like the barley chewy so I always overcook it until it has mushy texture which also helps with digestion. I then rinse it under warm water to remove the excess starch. Even better is to presoak the barley before cooking it. Drain and place in a large bowl.
2. While the barley is cooking boil the gizzards. Rinse and chop them into small pieces depending on your dog's size. Cook the spinach in water for about six minutes. Try not to overcook so you don't lose those nutrients.
3. Place the dried cranberries and safflower oil in your food processor and finely chop. (The oil is good for the skin and will keep the cranberries from sticking together).
4. Now just add all the ingredients into the bowl with the barley.
5. Thoroughly mix.

Prep Time: 20 minutes	Cook Time: 25 minutes	
Yields: 16 –1 cup servings	Calories: 193	Calories from fat: 27

chicken gumbo

The majority of Kirby's meals are homemade so I like to change it up to give him a variety of foods. This one has a lot of ingredients for their different healthy benefits but it's so easy to make. Granted it's not very pretty but the aroma while it's cooking is divine. Even out of the freezer, once thawed it has such a fresh smell.

Ingredients

- 4 lbs. chicken breasts
- 2 ½ cups chicken broth
- 1 (16 oz.) bag chopped frozen green beans
- 2 cups chopped yellow squash
- 1 (19 oz.) can rinsed lentils
- 1 cup blueberries
- 1 cup low fat cottage cheese
- ¼ cup ground flax seed
- ¼ cup dried parsley
- 2 tablespoons dried rosemary
- 1 teaspoon cayenne pepper
- 1 teaspoon ground turmeric
- 1 teaspoon ground ginger
- 1 teaspoon garlic powder
- ¼ teaspoon sea salt
- ¼ teaspoon ground egg shell
- 1 cup soaked barley

Directions

1. Boil the chicken breasts in water until cooked. Once cooled, discard the skin and bones. Save 2 1/2 cups of the chicken broth. Shred or chop the meat and set aside.
2. Place the remaining ingredients in a large Dutch oven or pot and cover with the reserved chicken broth. Heat over medium heat just until it begins to boil, then simmer covered on low heat for 2 to 3 hours until the veggies are soft.
3. Thoroughly mix in the shredded chicken.
4. Let cool and serve.

Prep Time: 35 minutes	Cook Time: 3 hours	
Yields: 14 –1 cup servings	Calories: 396	Calories from fat: 103

cottage cheese muttins

An easy dish to make ahead and freeze, these muffins have a light taste of cheese letting the meat shine through. Use ground chuck for a lean meal if you're watching your pups calories.

Ingredients

- 1 lb. ground beef
- 1 large egg
- 1 cup low fat cottage cheese
- 1 large chopped sweet potato
- 2 cups cooked brown rice
- ¼ teaspoon ground egg shell

Directions

1. Sweet potatoes are extremely hard to cut so I like to place them in the microwave about 20 seconds - just long enough to soften them so I can scoop out the flesh. Then shred in your food processor or blender.
2. Place all ingredients in a large bowl and thoroughly mix.
3. Spray muffin tin with light olive oil and fill each tin with the meat mixture.
4. Bake at 350 degrees for 45 minutes or until cooked through. Let cool and serve.

Prep Time: 15 minutes	Cook Time: 45 minutes	
Yields: 12 muffins	Calories: 208 each	Calories from fat: 36 each

Greek Lamb Patties

greek lamb patties

When we attend the local Cotton District Festival I always have to have a Greek gyro (pronounced yeer-oh). Kirby thinks he needs a few bites as he sits watching me eat. He is a perfect gentle dog as he patiently waits without making a sound so of course I do save him a few tasty bites he greedily devours.

The main ingredients in a gyro are the meat wrapped in pita bread. In Greece the gyro is typically made using pork or chicken, and sometimes veal with a yogurt type sauce. In the United States gyros are more typically made using lamb or a combination of beef and lamb. This is my canine interpretation of those delicious Americanized Greek gyros.

Ingredients

2 ¼ cups lamb
2 cups baby brown rice cereal
¼ cup plain Greek yogurt
2/3 cup lamb broth or chicken stock
1 large egg
¼ teaspoon ground turmeric
¼ teaspoon ground ginger
¼ teaspoon dried rosemary
¼ teaspoon ground egg shell

Directions

1. Braise lamb and shred. Place in large bowl.
2. Add remaining ingredients and thoroughly mix.
3. Fill muffin tins with meat mixture.
4. Bake at 350 degrees for 30 minutes or until lightly browned on edges.
5. Let cool.

Prep Time: 30 minutes	Cook Time: 30 minutes	
Yields: 12 muffins	Calories: 306 each	Calories from fat: 92 each

hamburger helper canine style

I used to make Hamburger Helper often for my children who loved it. I still make it once in a while now since it's easy and convenient. I like to provide Kirby a variety of meals so this is his canine variation. He has quite a few meals with potatoes or brown rice for his carbs so I always make this one with pasta for a nice change.

Ingredients

1 lb. ground beef
2 cups hot water
1 cup low fat or 2% milk
¾ cup plain Greek yogurt
1 ½ cups small pasta or 1 cup of brown rice
1 (15 oz.) can rinsed black beans
1 cup finely chopped veggies
1 tablespoon dried parsley
1 teaspoon garlic powder
1 teaspoon sea salt
½ teaspoon cayenne pepper
¼ teaspoon ground eggshell
2 tablespoons flour + 1 tablespoon water
1 cup shredded cheddar cheese

Directions

1. Brown ground beef in a large skillet or Dutch oven and sauté the veggies. I like to throw in a large green pepper.
2. Add the hot water, milk, yogurt, seasonings and pasta.
3. Add the whisked 2 tablespoons flour + 1 tablespoon water. This has the same thickening effect as cornstarch which should be avoided.
4. Bring to a boil. Cover and simmer on low about 12 minutes, stirring occasionally, until the pasta and beans are to an almost mushy texture.
5. Stir in the cheese and cover the pot again for a few minutes to allow the cheese to melt.
6. Remove from the heat and uncover. The sauce will thicken in about five minutes.

Prep Time: 10 minutes	Cook Time: 25 minutes	
Yields: 8 – 1 cup servings	Calories: 353	Calories from fat: 99

Little Italy Meatballs

little italy meatballs

Yes, I make these meatballs for Kirby. Yes, I've tasted them. Yes, I really like them. Seriously good, these little meatballs are yummy over pasta with a nice tomato sauce or as appetizers with a yogurt dip. The sardines add a nice smoky yet salty note. These are healthiest with ground turkey but feel free to use ground beef or pork. Kirby apparently doesn't really care what they are served with since he eats them first and then whatever is left in his bowl which can be as simple as a dollop of applesauce, low fat cottage cheese, or yogurt.

If you've never eaten sardines, let me tell you they taste a lot like tuna but with a smokiness. They're low in mercury and high in Omega-3 fatty acids. They're a healthy addition to any dog, or human, diet.

Ingredients

1 lb. ground turkey
1 (4.5 oz. can) sardines in tomato sauce
½ cup plain bread crumbs
1 large egg
2 tablespoons dried parsley
½ teaspoon garlic powder
½ teaspoon sea salt
¼ cup parmesan cheese
¼ teaspoon ground egg shell

Directions

1. In a medium bowl thoroughly mix all of the ingredients.
2. Using a cookie scoop, measure out the meatballs. Then spray a little oil on your hands to form into round balls.
3. Place on lined baking sheet.
4. Bake for 15 minutes at 350 degrees then turn broiler to high for another 3-5 minutes until golden brown.
5. Remove and let cool.

Prep Time: 10 minutes	Cook Time: 20 minutes	
Yields: 40 meatballs	Calories: 53 each	Calories from fat: 24 each

meaty muffins

This is one of the first canine meals I created and still one of Kirby's favorites! It's also one of the easiest to make - just mix and bake. These muffins are chock full of healthy ingredients and can be frozen for make ahead meals

Ingredients

½ cup cooked brown rice
1 ½ cups instant mashed potato flakes or 1 large finely chopped potato
1 ½ cups chopped carrots
1 lb. ground beef
3 large eggs
¼ teaspoon sea salt
¼ teaspoon ground egg shell
1 tablespoon extra light olive oil
½ cup old fashioned oats
1 cup fresh or frozen blueberries

Directions

1. Cook the brown rice according to package directions. I usually make two to four cups since it makes a nice side dish or an easy lunch to carry to work.
2. In a large bowl mix together all of the ingredients using your hands to thoroughly blend.
3. Spray muffin cups with olive oil and fill each one with some of the meat mixture patting down to make it firm.
4. Bake at 400 degrees for 40 minutes or until surface feels set.
5. Cool on a rack 10 minutes before removing from muffin tin.

Prep Time: 15 minutes	Cook Time: 40 minutes	
Yields: 18 muffins	Calories: 120 each	Calories from fat: 31 each

muttloaf

I love meatloaf and mashed potatoes with gravy. Talk about comfort food for the soul! I enjoy feeding Kirby different options so I thought why not a meatloaf of his own, hence muttloaf was born.

There really is no wrong way to make meatloaf. All you need is a pound of ground beef and a little imagination to come up with your own recipe. Kirby doesn't like to eat raw carrots so I try to implement them into his meals or treats but you can use any veggies. Using baby food gives me the liquid I need to blend the ingredients but you can chop some fresh veggies and add tomato paste or water. Flax seed is really good for Kirby's skin and coat but can be replaced with a few tablespoons of coconut oil for the same benefits. I use sun dried tomatoes for a chewy texture but you can use fresh or canned diced tomatoes.

Check my lists of Healthy Ingredients and Harmful Ingredients, then just use what you have in your refrigerator or pantry. Your pup will love it! Kirby and our fosters say Muttloaf is good stuff!

Ingredients

- 1 lb. ground beef
- 2 large eggs
- 2 cups old fashioned oats
- 2 teaspoons dried parsley
- 2 (3.5 oz.) jars natural carrots baby food
- ¼ cup ground flax seed
- ¼ teaspoon ground egg shell
- 1 cup diced sun dried tomatoes

Directions

1. Place all the ingredients in a large bowl and, using your hands, mix thoroughly.
2. Form into individual small loaves and place on greased rack of broiler pan.
3. Bake at 350 degrees for 45 minutes.
4. Let cool and serve.

Prep Time: 10 minutes	Cook Time: 45 minutes	
Yields: 8 loaves	Calories: 217 each	Calories from fat: 77 each

Sheperd's Pie

shepherd's pie

This classic savory pie is traditionally prepared from leftovers. Meat and vegetables are moistened with gravy, transferred to a pie plate, and topped with mashed potatoes. Since it's made from leftovers, feel free to use any ground meat, veggies, and seasonings which are deemed to be dog friendly.

Ingredients

1 lb. ground beef
½ cup chopped carrots
½ cup chopped green peas
½ cup plain bread crumbs
¼ teaspoon garlic powder
1 teaspoon dried parsley
¼ teaspoon sea salt
¼ teaspoon cayenne pepper
¼ teaspoon ground egg shell
1 large egg
1 1/3 cups cooked mashed potatoes
½ cup shredded cheddar cheese

Directions

1. Thoroughly combine all the ingredients except the mashed potatoes and cheese in a large bowl.
2. Divide the mixture evenly into 12 greased muffin tins. Use your fingers to pat down the bottom and sides of each cup to form a bowl.
3. Prepare the mashed potatoes. It's ok to use instant potatoes as long as they are 100% potato. The small amount of milk and butter won't hurt either unless your dog is lactose intolerant. In that case just omit them. Next add in your choice of cheese. I've used sharp cheddar cheese and feta cheese with good results. Pipe or spoon the potato mixture into the meat bowls.
4. Bake at 375 degrees for 15 to 20 minutes or until meat is thoroughly cooked.
5. Remove from oven and let rest for 15 minutes to set.
6. Remove to a baker's rack to cool.

Prep Time: 20 minutes	Cook Time: 15-20 minutes	
Yields: 12 pies	Calories: 137 each	Calories from fat: 43 each

southwestern chicken chili

Kirby loves food. Kirby loves spicy food. I love Kirby so I decided something with a tasty little kick would be just what he was craving. Something with a Southwestern flavor, something Bobby Flay would approve!

The black beans contribute 234 calories per serving but remember they are very low in saturated fat, cholesterol and sodium, a good source of protein, thiamin, magnesium, phosphorus and manganese, and an excellent source of dietary fiber and folate.

Ingredients

- 2 cups shredded cooked chicken
- 3 cups soaked barley
- 1 (14.5 oz.) can drained and rinsed black beans
- 3 teaspoons garlic powder
- ¼ teaspoon cayenne pepper
- ¼ teaspoon sea salt
- ¼ teaspoon ground egg shell
- 1 teaspoon dried parsley
- 1 cup chicken stock

Directions

1. Cook the barley using chicken stock in place of the water.
2. Kirby only likes black beans really mushy so I mince them but this isn't necessary.
3. Place all of the ingredients in a large bowl, add the seasonings, and mix thoroughly.
4. Let cool and serve.

You can use brown rice in place of the barley but it's a nice healthy change adding to the variety of foods your dog eats.

Prep Time: 20 minutes	Cook Time: 15 minutes	
Yields: 16 – 1 cup servings	Calories: 103 each	Calories from fat: 32

the carnivore's cake

It looks like a cake but it's really a meal for the carnivore in every dog! Yes, it is expensive at $5 for two filets but droolingly delectable for that very special occasion or event. I've always created a sweet pupcake for his barkday but, since he prefers savory over sweet, I went a different route for Kirby's very significant 5th barkday.

Aside from being expensive, it is so very easy. Have a special celebration or just want to pamper your pooch, this will surely do it!

Ingredients

    1 bacon wrapped beef filet
    1 cup cooked mashed potatoes
    cooked crumbled bacon

Directions

1. Prepare the mashed potatoes. I usually make mine from scratch with a couple of medium size potatoes, a little butter and milk. You can also use instant flakes as long as they are 100% potato.
2. Stir in the bacon.
3. Bake the filet following the directions on the package. I cook Kirby's at 350 degrees for twenty minutes for medium rare.
4. Let the meat cool and then place on the plate. Scoop cooled mashed potatoes into a bakers bag and squeeze onto the top of the meat like frosting a cupcake. You can use a zip lock bag by snipping a corner,
5. Take lots of pictures of your pup with his "cake" and then cut into bite size pieces.

Prep Time: 20 minutes	Cook Time: 20 minutes	
Yields: 1 serving	Calories: 648	Calories from fat: 295

turkey burgers

Kirby loves a healthy burger! These are made with turkey but any lean ground meat would work.

These can be formed into patties and cooked on the stove. If you're grilling then throw some on with your hamburgers (these are soft so cook on aluminum foil so they don't fall through) and freeze the remaining patties for next time.

Ingredients

1 lb. ground turkey
1 (12 oz.) bag broccoli slaw
2 Roma tomatoes or ½ cup tomato juice
½ cup plain bread crumbs
¼ cup parmesan cheese
1 large egg
¼ teaspoon ground egg shell

Directions

1. Purée or finely dice your veggies.
2. In a large bowl use your hands to thoroughly mix together all the ingredients.
3. Evenly fill each oil sprayed muffin tin with the meat mixture.
4. Bake at 400 degrees for 20 to 25 minutes.
5. Remove from the oven and let them sit for about ten minutes to firm up before removing.

If you can't find broccoli slaw in the produce section, chop up 4 cups of broccoli, carrots and cabbage.

Prep Time: 10 minutes	Cook Time: 25 minutes	
Yields: 12 burgers	Calories: 128 each	Calories from fat: 55 each

viva la venison

It's good to have friends! Especially hunting friends who bring us deer meat! This gamey protein is practically no fat and super healthy.

Ingredients

- 1 lb. ground venison
- 1 ½ cups old fashioned oats
- 1 large egg
- ¼ cup coconut milk
- 1 cup fresh or frozen blueberries
- ¼ cup dried parsley
- 2 tablespoons extra light olive oil
- ¼ teaspoon sea salt
- ½ teaspoon garlic powder
- ½ teaspoon cayenne pepper
- ¼ teaspoon ground egg shell

Directions

1. With your hands thoroughly mix all of the ingredients in a large bowl.
2. Evenly divide the mixture and pat down into oil sprayed mini loaf tin or muffin tin.
3. Bake at 350 degrees for 25 minutes or until meat is no longer pink.
4. Let cool and serve.

Prep Time: 10 minutes	Cook Time: 25 minutes	
Yields: 8 mini loaves	Calories: 231 each	Calories from fat: 104 each

grain free meals

Kirby doesn't have any problems with grains so he is able to eat a large variety of foods but I realize there are dogs who must avoid grains in their diet. If your dog tolerates grains feel free to add them to many of these recipes to stretch your budget.

Asian Fish Balls	208
Avocado Egg Salad	209
Bacon, Eggs & Quinoa	210
Beef Heart Soup	211
Breakfast Muffins	212
Canned Fish Stew	213
Chicken Gizzard Stew	214
Chicken Liver Meatballs	215
Chicken N Greens	216
Chicken, Quinoa & Kale	217
Chicken Salad	218
Cinnamon Beef Stew	219
Coconut Fish Soup	221
Country Roots Beef Stew	222
Hawaiian Burgers	223
Hearty Beef Stew	224
Hunter's Chicken Stew	225
Liver Dumplings	227
Loaves of Lamb	229
Monster Mashed Muttins	230
PB Scrambled Eggs	231
Polpette di Sarde	233
Roman Style Tripe	234
Sardine Parfait	235
Savory Scrambled Eggs	236
Savory Turkey Muttloaf	237
Scrambled Eggs & Tuna	239
Thanksgiving Dinner	241
The Fabulous Frittata	243
Tuna Salad	244
Venison Stew	245

asian fish balls

I'm always trying to think outside of the box when it comes to Kirby's meals and treats to give him a wide variety of flavors and textures. At a favorite Chinese buffet in all its glory was a soup filled with fish balls. I was already taking mental notes since the Kirbster very much loves fish and seafood.

A good fish ball should have an elastic (bouncy) and fluffy texture and a strong taste of fish. The basic ingredient is fish although flour and seasonings can also be used. Kirby likes catfish but any white fish such as cod or tilapia is recommended.

Ingredients

   2 lbs. catfish fillets
   1 teaspoon sea salt
   ¼ teaspoon cayenne pepper
   ¼ teaspoon ground turmeric
   1 teaspoon dried parsley
   ½ teaspoon ground eggshell

Directions

1. Make sure there are no bones and then finely chop the fish.
2. Place in a large bowl and add the seasonings using your hands to thoroughly mix.
3. Now gather up the mixture with your hands and "slap it" back down into the bowl. Repeat this several times noting that too little slapping makes them mushy while too much slapping makes them tough. They should be bouncy and springy to the bite which in true Asian cuisine would take sixty to seventy slaps. However, since this dish is for my dog, I slap them maybe five or six times
4. Form into small balls.
5. Heat water to boiling in a medium size pot. If you have dog friendly fish stock, that's even better!
6. Once the water is boiling drop the balls into the water. They are done when they float to the top. Scoop out onto a plate and let cool.

To serve, or freeze, place several fish balls in a small bowl or container and add 1/4 cup of the "fish flavored water" to each container before freezing.

Prep Time: 10 minutes	Cook Time: 3-5 minutes	
Yields: 48 small balls	Calories: 26 each	Calories from fat: 13 each

avocado egg salad

I love avocados. Kirby loves avocados. One of my fave lunches is a sliced avocado with cottage cheese, often times I make my deviled eggs with avocado instead of mayonnaise, and I've been making this egg salad for years.

For the longest time it has been warned that avocados were toxic for dogs but now holistic veterinarians, along with various credible websites, are touting their safety. It's the skin and pit which pose the problem as they contain persin which can cause digestive upsets and heart problems. Kirby has been eating them since he was a pup with no side effects whatsoever.

If you still feel uncomfortable then make it just for yourself and give your pup a bite or two. No adverse reaction? Then next time give him a little more. Eventually you'll be splitting the recipe, half for the humans and half for the dogs. It's that good!

Ingredients

12 large eggs
2 small pitted and peeled avocados
2 tablespoon plain greek yogurt
1 tablespoon fresh lemon juice
¼ teaspoon ground turmeric
¼ teaspoon sea salt

Directions

1. Boil the eggs, peel and chop. Set aside.
2. Use a blender or food processor to thoroughly combine the remaining ingredients.
3. Mix into the chopped eggs.

This will keep for up to five days in the refrigerator.

Prep Time: 15 minutes	Cook Time: 20 minutes	
Yields: 12 – 1/2 cup servings	Calories: 132	Calories from fat: 98

bacon, eggs & quinoa

We love to eat breakfast for dinner and Kirby does too. We usually enjoy eggs, bacon and grits. Grits are made from corn which he can't have so I decided eggs, bacon and quinoa (which I love to eat with some lemon juice and sea salt) would be a good combo.

Ingredients

- 3 cups cooked quinoa
- 12 slices turkey bacon
- 3 large eggs
- 1 cup unsweetened applesauce

Directions

1. Cook the bacon and crumble into small pieces.
2. Scramble the eggs remembering they need to be cooked completely.
3. Add the bacon, eggs, and applesauce to the quinoa.
4. Mix well and serve warm.

This should keep in the refrigerator for three to four days.

To cook 3 cups of quinoa

Ingredients

- 1 cup quinoa
- 2 cups cold water
- ¼ teaspoon sea salt

Directions

1. Soak the quinoa in enough water to cover for five minutes then strain. This helps it cook more evenly and removes any residue. (You can purchase pre-rinsed quinoa).
2. Next place the quinoa in a 2 quart pot and add the water and salt. Bring to a boil.
3. Cover with tight fitting lid and simmer for fifteen minutes.
4. Remove from heat and let sit five minutes with lid on.
5. Fluff with a fork and pour into a large bowl.

Prep Time: 5 minutes	Cook Time: 20 minutes	
Yields: 5 – 1/2 cup servings	Calories: 460	Calories from fat: 87

beef heart soup

Beef heart has been called the poor man's steak (under $3.00 for a 3 lb. heart) as it has a burst of extra meaty flavor. Since it's one of the purest cuts of muscle, it is really dense and tender. It's very similar to steak, roasts and ground beef but has a higher protein content.

Ingredients

- 1 (3 lb.) beef heart
- 2 cups chicken stock or water
- 3 chopped small sweet potatoes
- 2 chopped celery stalks
- 1 chopped turnip
- 3 chopped small yellow squash
- 3 chopped carrots
- 2 tablespoons extra light olive oil
- 2 teaspoons garlic powder
- ½ teaspoon sea salt
- ½ teaspoon cayenne pepper
- ½ teaspoon ground turmeric
- 1 ½ teaspoons ground egg shell

Directions

1. Prepare the beef heart cutting away the tough, fatty top of the heart containing valves and tendons. Soak in cold, salted water for 1 to 2 hours so the excess blood will be rinsed away. Next carefully cut away the membrane and fat from the meat getting as close as possible. Finally cut the heart into strips, and then into 1 inch cubes.
2. Heat the olive oil in a Dutch oven or large stockpot over medium heat and lightly brown the cubes of meat.
3. Add the vegetables to the pot. Stir in the seasonings and pour in the chicken stock. Bring to a boil and then reduce the heat to simmer for two to three hours until the vegetables are tender.

You could stretch it out by adding a grain such as barley or a bean such as black beans.

Prep Time: 2 hours	Cook Time: 2-3 hours	
Yields: 6 – 1 cup servings	Calories: 545	Calories from fat: 144

breakfast muffins

These grain free muffins are always a nice change for those special mornings. You can pick and choose the ingredients your pup likes best for the filling. For less calories try using turkey sausage. Any finely chopped veggie will work. Try different cheeses - mozzarella, parmesan, goat, and feta. The possibilities are endless making this an easy favorite for both humans and canines. I prepare it in 2 steps but you can do it all at one time.

Filling Ingredients

1 lb. ground mild sausage
¼ teaspoon cayenne pepper
¼ teaspoon ground egg shell
1 cup chopped frozen spinach
½ cup shredded cheddar cheese

Egg Mixture Ingredients

8 large eggs
¼ cup low fat or 2% milk
½ tablespoon safflower oil

Directions

1. In a large pan cook the sausage. When almost cooked, stir in the cayenne pepper. Drain and place in a medium size bowl.
2. Finely chop the spinach and remove any excess moisture with paper towels.
3. Stir the spinach and cheddar cheese into the meat.
4. Evenly spoon this mixture into an oiled muffin tin, cover with foil, and place in the refrigerator.
5. Whisk together the eggs, milk, and oil in a two cup measuring cup, cover with foil, and place in the refrigerator.
6. In the morning preheat the oven to 350 degrees. Pour an even amount of the egg mixture into each muffin tin.
7. Throw some extra cheddar cheese on top if you want.
8. Bake for 16 minutes. Remove and let cool for 10 minutes to firm up.
9. Run a flat knife around the edges to remove the muffins.

Prep Time: 20 minutes	Cook Time: 16 minutes	
Yields: 12 muffins	Calories: 195 each	Calories from fat: 140 each

canned fish stew

Kirby is a carnivore. He loves meat... beef, venison, fowl, and fish. I have yet to discover what his favorite fish is as he greedily devours anchovies, sardines, herring, salmon, mackerel, tilapia, cod, whiting, catfish... The dog loves fish!

I knew I couldn't go wrong as long as the star of the dish was fish so really I just started throwing together what I had in the pantry. This is so easy and tasty your dog will discover his or her "inner cat" in no time.

Ingredients

- 2 (14.75 oz.) cans salmon
- 3 (15 oz.) cans mackerel
- 2 to 3 tablespoons coconut oil
- 1 ½ cups broccoli slaw
- 3 chopped small sweet potatoes
- 1 (14.5 oz.) can drained sweet peas
- 3 cups chicken stock
- 2 (13.66 oz.) cans coconut milk
- 1 teaspoon garlic powder
- 1 teaspoon ground ginger
- 1 teaspoon dill seed
- ¼ teaspoon ground egg shell

Directions

1. Finely chop the broccoli slaw and peeled sweet potatoes. Kirby doesn't like sweet peas so I chop them up to hide them.
2. In a Dutch oven or large pot sauté the veggies in the coconut oil over medium low heat for 20 to 30 minutes until tender.
3. Pour in the chicken stock and coconut milk. Add the seasonings.
4. Drain and crush, or remove, the spiny bones in the salmon and mackerel. Add to the pot.
5. Let simmer until warmed through.

If you can't find broccoli slaw in the produce section, chop up some broccoli, carrots and cabbage.

Prep Time: 15 minutes	Cook Time: 45 minutes	
Yields: 15 – 1 cup servings	Calories: 495	Calories from fat: 297

chicken gizzard stew

Gizzards are an organ found in the digestive tract of a chicken used to grind up the foods the bird eats. They're considered a delicacy in certain cultures and provide a healthy dose of protein, iron, zinc and Vitamin B12. They are high in cholesterol so Kirby can have one meal a week.

This is an easy stew you can throw together in a few hours. Even easier is to throw it all in your crock pot, plug it in, and come back later to a fully cooked stew. Sometimes I'll add some leftover shredded chicken meat. Adding some rice or pasta can help stretch out the meals.

Ingredients

2 to 3 lbs. chicken gizzards
3 tablespoons extra light olive oil
4 cups chopped veggies
4 cups chicken stock
1 tablespoon coconut flour
¼ teaspoon ground eggshell

Directions

1. Clean and chop the gizzards. In a large Dutch oven or pot heat the olive oil and cook the gizzards until no longer pink.
2. Add the chicken stock and veggies. I use different bags of assorted frozen veggies; one of my favorite's being Birdseye Normandy Blend containing broccoli, cauliflower, carrots, yellow squash, and zucchini. Reduce the heat and let simmer until the veggies are tender.

To thicken the broth scoop out a cup and mix in one tablespoon flour, then pour back into the pot.

Prep Time: 15 minutes	Cook Time: 2 hours	
Yields: 12 – 1 cup servings	Calories: 115	Calories from fat: 44

chicken liver meatballs

Chicken livers are an excellent source of high quality protein and a rich source of Vitamins A, D and virtually all of the B vitamins. They are also relatively inexpensive so stock up and bake these easy meatballs. I save a lot of time when making meatballs by using a cookie dough scoop. They may not be perfectly round but Kirby doesn't seem to mind.

Ingredients

- 1 to 2 lb. chicken livers
- 1 chopped green pepper
- 1 cup chopped spinach
- 2 teaspoons garlic powder
- 1 teaspoon extra light olive oil
- ¼ cup dried parsley
- ¼ teaspoon sea salt
- ¼ teaspoon cayenne pepper
- 1 large egg
- ¼ teaspoon ground egg shell
- ½ cup dried cranberries
- ½ cup coconut flour

Directions

1. Rinse and pat dry the chicken livers. Heat the olive oil in a medium size pan and sauté the chicken livers until the outsides are a light brown. Remove from heat and let cool.
2. Cook the green pepper and spinach over medium heat. Stir in the garlic powder and remove pan from heat.
3. Puree the cooked mixture in a blender and pour into a medium size bowl. Add the remaining ingredients and thoroughly combine.
4. Add more flour if needed to form small meatballs. Coconut flour absorbs a lot of moisture so if using a different flour use 1/3 cup.
5. Place on a lined baking sheet and bake at 350 degrees for 15 to 20 minutes until crispy and browned.
6. Let cool for 15 minutes to firm up.

Prep Time: 30 minutes	Cook Time: 20 minutes	
Yields: 36 – 2" meatballs	Calories: 42 each	Calories from fat: 15 each

chicken n greens

Just three ingredients plus whatever seasonings you want to use that are dog friendly! So how did this simple recipe come about? I had run out of Kirby's frozen meals and needed to whip up something simple and easy with what I had on hand. This is a healthy and tasty dish made with love. It's also a fan favorite!

Ingredients

4 chicken leg quarters
1 (18 oz.) bag chopped frozen turnip greens
7 (4 oz.) jars natural baby food - 3 carrots, 2 peas, 2 squash
¼ teaspoon sea salt
¼ teaspoon cayenne pepper
¼ teaspoon ground turmeric
¼ teaspoon ground egg shell
1 cup chicken stock

Directions

1. Boil the chicken in a Dutch oven or large stock pot. Remove and let cool. (Save the liquid) Once cool enough to handle, discard the skin and bones. Shred the meat.
2. Rinse out the Dutch oven and add the cooked chicken back in. Add all of the remaining ingredients except the saved chicken stock.
3. Mix thoroughly and add the chicken stock.
4. Heat over low heat stirring occasionally until the turnip greens have cooked. It will have the texture of a chili rather than a soup.
5. Let cool and serve.

Any greens will do - kale, spinach.

Any natural baby food veggies are acceptable.

Prep Time: 10 minutes	Cook Time: 1 hour	
Yields: 9 – 1 cup servings	Calories: 162	Calories from fat: 34

chicken, quinoa & kale

Want a powerhouse meal for your dog that's chock full of beneficial ingredients and flavor? Quinoa, which has a mild, nutty flavor, is often referred to as the mother of all grains. In fact it is not a grain but a seed from a vegetable related to Swiss chard, spinach, and beets. It's high in fiber and protein while also packing in iron and potassium. One half cup of quinoa has 14 grams of protein and 6 grams of fiber. This superfood is naturally gluten-free. Kale is a nutrient dense leafy green containing beta carotene, calcium, vitamin C, vitamin K, and lutein. It has anti-inflammatory properties, is full of anti-oxidants and healthy flavonoids, and is believed to help prevent cancer.

I use chicken legs for a change but you can use thighs or breasts. You could use water in place of the chicken stock but you're losing some excellent flavor and nutrients. If you don't make your own stock, be sure to check the label of purchased stock to avoid onions which are toxic for dogs.

Ingredients

10 chicken legs
2 cups quinoa
1 (16 oz.) bag fresh kale
chicken stock
¼ teaspoon ground egg shell

Directions

1. In a Dutch oven or large stockpot boil the chicken legs until the meat is almost falling off. Drain and save the stock for cooking the quinoa and kale. Remove the bones and skin. Shred the meat and set aside.
2. Cook the quinoa. Combine 2 cups quinoa with 4 cups of the chicken stock in the Dutch oven or large pot and bring to a boil. Cover, reduce heat to low and simmer for 15 minutes or until all liquid is absorbed. Remove from heat and let sit for 5 minutes. Uncover and mix in the chicken meat.
3. Finely chop the kale for better digestion and sauté in a pan with 1/2 cup of the reserved chicken stock. Stir in the ground eggshell. Mix into the quinoa chicken mixture.

Prep Time: 20 minutes	Cook Time: 45 minutes	
Yields: 18 – 1 cup servings	Calories: 234	Calories from fat: 65

chicken salad

I love chicken salad by itself or in a sandwich. I like to roast my own chickens with Dr. Pepper but sometimes I cheat by purchasing a roasted chicken at the store. The meat goes in the salad while the carcass goes in the freezer for future chicken stock. Often times I'll make my basic chicken salad then divide it into two bowls - one for Kirby as is and one for us with added grapes and pecans which are toxic for him.

Ingredients

- 1 roasted chicken
- 5 large boiled eggs
- 1 cup homemade ranch dressing

Directions

1. Remove the bones and skin and shred the chicken meat.
2. Peel and chop the boiled eggs.
3. Mix everything in a medium size bowl and chill.

homemade ranch dressing

Ingredients

- 3/4 cup plain greek yogurt
- 1 teaspoon dill weed
- 1 teaspoon garlic powder
- 6 tablespoons extra light olive oil
- 2 tablespoons parmesan cheese

Directions

1. Thoroughly blend all of the ingredients except for the light olive oil in a small blender or food processor.
2. While blending drizzle in the oil very slowly one tablespoon at a time so that it emulsifies.

This will keep up to one week in the refrigerator.

Prep Time: 30 minutes	Cook Time: 10 minutes	
Yields: 8 – 1/2 cup servings	Calories: 279	Calories from fat: 179
	(includes the ranch dressing)	

cinnamon beef stew

This is a savory twist on traditional beef stew based on Stifado (stee-FAH-though), a Greek stew that is typically made with a fair amount of onions, wine, tomatoes, and cinnamon. I've removed the onions and wine since those are huge no-no's for dogs. Also, unlike a typical beef stew, this one doesn't have potatoes so it's a little more on the soupy side which is ok since dogs really need about 70% moisture in their daily diet.

What this dish lacks in appearance, it makes up for in flavor. It takes a little extra effort but the aromas and flavor are well worth it. Actually it's a meal you can share with your pups. Feel free to add whatever veggies you have on hand as long as they are dog friendly. To make it a little easier, once you have browned the meat and sautéed the veggies and tomato paste, place everything in your crock pot. Cook on low for 10-12 hours or high for 3 to 4 hours adding more water or stock if it appears too dry.

Ingredients

- 2 ½ pounds beef stew meat
- 2 tablespoons coconut flour
- 3 tablespoons coconut oil
- 2 cups chopped carrots
- 2 cups chopped kale
- 2 minced garlic cloves or 1 teaspoon garlic powder
- 2 tablespoons tomato paste or 1 (14.4 oz.) can diced tomatoes
- 1 cup bone (beef) broth or chicken broth
- 3 to 5 cups water
- 1 teaspoon sea salt
- 2 bay leaves
- 1 teaspoon dried rosemary
- 1 teaspoon ground thyme
- 2 teaspoons ground cinnamon
- 1 teaspoon ground egg shell
- quinoa, brown rice or pasta (optional)

Directions

1. This goes fast so it's best to have all of your ingredients ready beforehand. Cut the stew meat into one inch cubes. Lightly dust the meat with a few tablespoons of coconut flour. Finely chop the vegetables and mince the garlic. Gather all your seasonings in a small bowl.
2. In a large pot or Dutch oven melt the coconut oil over medium-high heat. Add the meat in batches and sear on all sides. Remove the browned pieces to a bowl. Repeat until all of the meat is cooked. Do not drain any of the juice from the meat from the pot.

the canine chef cookbook

3. Add the carrots, kale, and garlic to the juice in the pot and sauté for about 2 minutes. Add the tomato paste or diced tomatoes and stir for another minute.
4. Add the broth and scrape any brown bits that may be stuck on the bottom. Keep stirring until the mixture starts to thicken.
5. Add 3 cups water and the seasonings.
6. Bring to a boil and add the cooked meat and drippings back in. Then reduce the heat to a low simmer, cover, and cook 2 to 3 hours until the beef is very tender.
7. Once it's done remove and discard the bay leaves.

I like to add 3 cups of quinoa which requires another 2 cups of beef broth during the last hour and let it cook with the stew but this is totally optional. You could also add pasta or brown rice. Whichever you choose, be sure it is cooked beyond al dente for easy digestion.

Prep Time: 30 minutes	Cook Time: 2-3 hours	
Yields: 14 – 1 cup servings	Calories: 197	Calories from fat: 74

coconut fish soup

Kirby eats a lot of chicken and red meat. Fish is another healthy option he dearly loves. I happened to catch some catfish on sale one time which he loved so that's what I tend to use but any white fish would work. Kirby laps up the broth but you can omit the water if you want a thicker stew.

Ingredients

   2 lbs. catfish nuggets
   3 chopped small sweet potatoes
   1 (12 oz.) bag broccoli slaw
   2 cups green peas
   2 (13.5 oz.) cans coconut milk
   3 cups water
   1 (5 oz.) bag dried mixed berries (cranberries, blueberries, cherries)
   2 tablespoons coconut flour
   1 teaspoon garlic powder
   1 teaspoon ground ginger
   ¼ teaspoon ground egg shell

Directions

1. Finely chop the broccoli slaw.
2. Mix the dried berries with two tablespoons flour which will help keep them from clumping together, and finely chop. I use coconut flour but any flour will work.
3. Rinse and dry the fish, deboning if needed, then cut into small pieces.
4. In a large pot bring the coconut milk and water to a slow boil. Add the sweet potatoes, broccoli slaw, peas, dried berries, and seasonings.
5. Simmer over low heat for ten minutes, stirring occasionally.
6. Add the fish and let simmer for twenty minutes or until fish and veggies are thoroughly cooked.
7. Let cool and serve.

If you can't find broccoli slaw in the produce section, chop up 4 cups of broccoli, carrots and cabbage.

Prep Time: 30 minutes	Cook Time: 35 minutes	
Yields: 12 – 1 cup servings	Calories: 272	Calories from fat: 149

country roots beef stew

There's nothing more nourishing and filling on a cold day than beef stew. This stew is all about root veggies which are low in fat and high in nutrient value. It really doesn't matter how much of each veggie you use, just start chopping and throw it in the pot. Choose any of the following root veggies - carrots, celery, beets, yams, sweet potatoes, parsnip, and turnips. DO NOT USE onions or mushrooms as these are highly toxic to dogs.

Ingredients

- 1 lb. beef stew meat
- 2 chopped large potatoes
- 3 chopped small turnips
- 4 chopped large carrots
- 1 (28 oz.) can undrained crushed tomatoes
- 2 tablespoons extra light olive oil
- ¼ teaspoon ground egg shell
- ½ teaspoon garlic powder
- ½ teaspoon sea salt
- 2 teaspoons dried parsley
- ¼ teaspoon finely chopped basil
- ¼ teaspoon ground oregano

Directions

1. Using a Dutch oven or large oven-safe pot, brown the meat in the olive oil.
2. Add the chopped veggies and crushed tomatoes to the pot.
3. Add enough water to cover everything. Mix well.
4. Cover and cook in the oven at 350 degrees for two or more hours until the meat and veggies are tender.
5. During the cooking process if you want to thicken the stew, scoop out some of the broth in a cup, mix in some flour, and then pour it back into the stew.
6. Remove from the oven and let cool before serving.

Prep Time: 20 minutes	Cook Time: 2 to 10 hours	
Yields: 12 – 1 cup servings	Calories: 178	Calories from fat: 43

hawaiian burgers

Traditionally these burgers have pineapple slices on top and are served on a bun. I decided to put the pineapple inside the burger. I cut way back on the barbeque sauce and added an egg to help bind the meat. The patty just looked so naked sitting there without a bun so I decided to whip up a quick, healthy sauce with the extra crushed pineapple.

Kirby doesn't get much pork since it's so fatty so this a special meal served only once in a while. He gets just one while I freeze the rest for later.

Ingredients

1 pound ground pork
½ teaspoon ground ginger
1/8 teaspoon cayenne pepper
½ cup fresh or canned crushed pineapple
1 tablespoon plain barbecue sauce (no onions)
1 large egg
¼ teaspoon ground egg shell

Directions

1. Using your hands mix all of the ingredients together in a bowl until just combined. Don't knead too much or the burgers will be tough. If using canned pineapple be sure to drain the juice saving some for the sauce.
2. Gently press equal amounts in an oil sprayed muffin tin, with a slight indentation in the middle (the burgers will contract as they cook so the indentation helps keep the burgers from bulging in the middle too much).
3. Bake at 350 degrees for 25 - 30 minutes.

the sauce

3 to 4 tablespoons plain greek yogurt
2 to 3 tablespoons crushed pineapple
1 tablespoon pineapple juice

1. Place yogurt in a small bowl and stir in crushed pineapple and juice.
2. Mix with spoon and ladle onto plate or over patty.

Prep Time: 10 minutes	Cook Time: 30 minutes	
Yields: 6 patties	Calories: 140	Calories from fat: 31

hearty beef stew

We all know a good hearty stew can warm and nourish the body in a comforting way. This hearty stew brimming with meat and veggies will satisfy the pickiest eater, and since your dog wants what you want, you'll be assured he's eating a healthy meal made from human grade ingredients. This smells so good, why not grab some thick crusty bread, ladle a bowl for yourself, and enjoy a hearty meal with your furkid!

Ingredients

- 2 lbs. beef stew meat
- 2 tablespoons extra light olive oil
- 3 cups bone (beef) broth
- 3 tablespoons coconut flour
- 1 ½ teaspoons garlic powder
- 1 teaspoon sea salt
- ¼ teaspoon cayenne pepper
- ½ teaspoon ground rosemary
- ½ teaspoon ground egg shell
- 3 to 4 medium chopped potatoes
- 2 cups chopped broccoli florets
- 4 to 5 chopped carrots
- 3 small chopped yellow squash
- 1 red apple, peeled, cored and chopped

Directions

1. Cut the meat into 1 inch cubes and place in a large dutch oven.
2. Add the olive oil and brown the meat over medium heat until most of the pink is gone.
3. Whisk the flour into the bone broth and add to the pot.
4. Add the garlic, ground eggshell, and seasonings.
5. Stir, cover, and simmer for about 30 minutes until the meat is no longer pink and the broth has thickened up a little bit.
6. Toss in the veggies and apple and continue to let simmer for about an hour and a half or until the vegetables reach the desired soft texture.
7. Let cool and serve.

Prep Time: 30 minutes	Cook Time: 2 hours	
Yields: 14 – 1 cup servings	Calories: 220	Calories from fat: 60

hunter's chicken stew

The Italian fable behind this dish is there was a hunter who was determined not to come home empty handed to his hungry children. Luckily he caught an escaped rabbit of a neighboring farmer and on the way home foraged for some wild herbs to go with it. Over the years hunter's stew became a dish using whatever was on hand in the kitchen. Since I don't have any rabbit (yet) I grab a chicken from the freezer.

This recipe takes a bit of work but it's a meal everyone can share.

Ingredients

1 whole cut up chicken
sea salt and cayenne pepper
8 bay leaves
2 teaspoons dried parsley
2 teaspoons finely chopped mint
¼ teaspoon garlic powder
¼ teaspoon ground egg shell
2 cups chicken broth
flour for dusting
2 tablespoons extra light olive oil
6 chopped anchovies
½ cup pitted and chopped black olives
1 (28 oz.) can stewed tomatoes
2 to 3 chopped carrots
1 chopped green pepper
1 chopped red pepper

Directions

1. Remove the skin and place the chicken pieces in a container with a cover. Season with the sea salt, cayenne pepper, parsley, mint, and garlic powder.
2. Pour the chicken stock over the chicken. Add the bay leaves, Cover and let marinate for at least an hour in the refrigerator, but preferably overnight.
3. Remove the chicken saving the marinade. Pat dry with paper towels and coat with flour shaking off any excess.
4. Heat the olive oil in a large Dutch oven or oven proof pot over medium heat. Cook the chicken 5 minutes on each side until golden brown. Remove and set aside.

5. Add the anchovies, olives, tomatoes, carrots and green peppers to the pot. Add the chicken back in. Pour the reserved marinade in and stir to blend everything.
6. Bring to a slow boil and cover.
7. Transfer to the oven and bake at 350 degrees for 1 hour.
8. Remove the bay leaves and chicken pieces. Debone and cut the chicken into bite-size pieces or shred the meat. Stir the meat back into the pot.
9. Serve alone or with whole wheat pasta or brown rice.

Prep Time: 70 minutes	Cook Time: 1 hour	
Yields: 9 – 1 cup servings	Calories: 170	Calories from fat: 58

liver dumplings

Let's face it, dogs love liver and dogs love bacon so these combine the best of both worlds for the ultimate doggie meatball. Serve them alone, with a dollop of plain Greek yogurt, over rice or pasta, or over mashed veggies like sweet potatoes or green beans.

Ingredients

- 1 cup calf liver
- 1 lb. ground beef
- 1 (2.5 oz.) bag real bacon bits
- ½ cup bone (beef) broth
- 1 large egg
- ½ teaspoon garlic powder
- ¼ teaspoon sea salt
- ¼ teaspoon cayenne pepper
- ½ teaspoon ground egg shell

Directions

1. Break up the liver in a food processor but don't completely puree it.
2. Place in a large bowl and thoroughly mix together with the remaining ingredients. If you want to bulk up the meatballs even more you can add about a cup of whole oats or cooked brown rice.
3. Shape into 1 inch meatballs. I usually use a cookie scoop to get a uniform size but using your hands is just as easy. They are a bit on the loose side but they do firm up as they bake.
4. Bake on a paper or foil lined baking sheet with sides to catch the juices at 350 degrees for about 30 minutes.
5. Remove to a rack to cool placing paper towels underneath to catch the drippings.
6. Once they have cooled use a dull knife or spoon to scrape off any remaining fat drippings.

A meal for a small dog would be 3 meatballs with a side of yogurt or a veggie. Replacing the ground beef with ground chuck will reduce the calories to 12 with 6 from fat.

Prep Time: 30 minutes	Cook Time: 20 minutes	
Yields: 36 balls	Calories: 66 each	Calories from fat: 20 each

Loaves of Lamb

loaves of lamb

Kirby enjoys kibble with lamb not to mention I always end up having to share my lamb gyros with him so I decided to create a meal for him with ground lamb. It's an easy dish to make but plan ahead for the long cooking times for the squash and the loaves themselves. The aroma wafting from the oven keeps Kirby in or near the kitchen the entire time just hoping for a bite!

Ingredients

1 lb. ground lamb
1 cup cooked butternut squash
½ cup ricotta cheese
1 cup crushed tomatoes
1 chopped red bell pepper
1 teaspoon garlic powder
¼ teaspoon cayenne pepper
1 teaspoon finely chopped mint
3 tablespoons dried parsley
¼ teaspoon ground egg shell
2 tablespoons extra light olive oil

Directions

1. In large bowl thoroughly combine all of the ingredients. I just use my hands to really work together all of this goodness.
2. Place equal portions in oil sprayed mini loaf tins.
3. Bake at 350 degrees for about 1 hour, 15 minutes until cooked through or reaches an internal temp of at least 160 degrees.
4. Remove to a bakers rack and let cool.

These loaves have a very soft texture but will firm up somewhat as they cool. You could add whole oats to the mix before cooking for firmer loaves but I like these to be grain free.

You can substitute the butternut squash with cooked sweet potato or pumpkin puree.

Prep Time: 20 minutes	Cook Time: 2 hours	
Yields: 8 mini loaves	Calories: 184 each	Calories from fat: 81 each

monster mashed muttins

It was nearing Halloween and that song "Do The Monster Mash" was in my head so it was no surprise I reached for the box of instant mashed potato flakes when concocting this recipe. It was a hit with both the Kirbster and our current foster boy. In fact, they each received one muffin until they both began begging for another. I gave in.

Ingredients

- 1 lb. ground beef
- 2 cups instant mashed potato flakes
- 1 (8 oz.) can drained and pureed asparagus
- 1 (4 oz.) jar natural squash baby food
- 1 cup shredded carrots
- 2 large eggs
- ¼ teaspoon ground egg shell

Directions

1. In a large bowl thoroughly mix together all the ingredients.
2. Evenly pat mixture into oil sprayed muffin tins.
3. Bake at 350 degrees for 45 minutes or until fully cooked.
4. Let cool and remove from muffin tin.

Prep Time: 10 minutes	Cook Time: 45 minutes	
Yields: 12 muffins	Calories: 120 each	Calories from fat: 28 each

pb scrambled eggs

This is something I whip up now and then for Kirby and myself. It's one of those strange concoctions you accidentally make out of necessity. I wanted scrambled eggs one morning but I was out of cheese. Plain scrambled eggs just seemed too boring so I began searching my cupboards.

Peanut butter? Mmmm, why not? I love it with jelly, love it in ice cream, and I can't ever resist a Reece's cup. I've been known to eat a spoonful now and then. So why not in eggs? I had plenty of eggs so I could scrap it if it turned out bad. But guess what? It was really good. So really this is my basic recipe for scrambled eggs when you don't have cheese.

Ingredients

1 tablespoon unsalted butter
2 large eggs
2 tablespoons natural peanut butter
1 teaspoon finely chopped herb (optional)
sea salt

Directions

1. Lightly whip the eggs to aerate until a creamy light yellow.
2. Whip in the peanut butter just until blended.
3. Add the fresh herb. This is optional and really not necessary. I sometimes like using parsley, but prefer basil. If Kirby has a preference he hasn't indicated what it might be. Mint doesn't work with this combo for me but you may like it. Also remember dogs cannot eat sage or chives. Make sure whatever herb you use is dog friendly!
4. Melt the butter in a non-stick sauce pan over low heat. Pour in the eggs working them with a spatula until almost cooked. (They will continue cooking from the residual heat). Remove from heat and sprinkle a little sea salt over them.

Taste and be amazed! Remember peanut butter is fattening so don't feed this too often.

Prep Time: 10 minutes	Cook Time: 10 minutes	
Yields: 4 servings	Calories: 107	Calories from fat: 82

Polpette Di Sarde

polpette di sarde

Kirby loves sardines which are high in omega-3 fatty acids and a good source of vitamin D, calcium, B12, and protein. This popular Italian dish from Sicily translates to Balls of Sardines and is often served with a simple tomato sauce. When shopping choose quality brands and pay attention to the variety of flavored sauces they come packed in. Use the ones packed in olive oil or tomato sauce not packed in mustard or pepper sauces. Kirby enjoys a meal of three meatballs with a smidge of tomato sauce. This is a classic meal you can share with your dog!

Ingredients

2 (3.75 oz.) cans sardines packed in light olive oil
2 large eggs
1 ¼ cups instant mashed potato flakes
2 tablespoons parmesan cheese
¼ teaspoon garlic powder
¼ cup dried parsley
¼ teaspoon sea salt
¼ teaspoon cayenne pepper
1/8 teaspoon ground egg shell
tomato sauce (optional)

Directions

1. Pour the sardines with the oil into a medium size bowl and mash them up.
2. Add the remaining ingredients and thoroughly mix.
3. I use a small cookie scoop but you can easily form small balls with your hands.
4. Place the meatballs in an oiled baking dish.
5. Bake at 400 degrees about 20 minutes or until lightly browned.
6. Let cool and serve. Pour the tomato sauce over the meatballs to complete the dish.

Pasta would make a good base if you want to stretch out the servings.

Prep Time: 20 minutes	Cook Time: 20 minutes	
Yields: 24 balls	Calories: 45 each	Calories from fat: 23 each

roman style tripe

Tripe, the cow's stomach, is considered a delicacy in many countries. Holistic veterinarians highly recommend raw, green tripe for its amazing benefits. I'm not prepared to venture that far so using bleached tripe is my first baby step in that direction. Even though this is made with human grade ingredients it's a meal I'm not tasting but I can say Kirby loves it since he literally inhales it. I know this can be somewhat hard to "stomach" but it's a very healthy meal. To be honest I only make this meal two to three times a year on days I can leave the back door open. The vinegar tones down the smell but it's worse than liver.

Ingredients

- 2 pounds honeycomb tripe
- ½ cup white vinegar
- 1 teaspoon pure vanilla extract
- 2 tablespoons extra light olive oil
- 1 medium chopped green pepper
- 2 teaspoons garlic powder
- 2 cups pureed tomatoes
- 1 teaspoon finely chopped mint
- ½ teaspoon ground egg shell
- ¼ cup parmesan cheese

Directions

1. Trim any pieces of solid fat from the tripe and wash the tripe thoroughly under cold running water.
2. In a large pot combine the tripe, vinegar, vanilla and enough water to cover the tripe by 2 inches. Bring to a boil, reduce to a simmer, and cook until the tripe is very tender, about 1 to 1 ¼ hours, replenishing the water as necessary.
3. Drain the tripe and let cool.
4. Scrape both sides of the tripe with the back of a knife to remove as many flecks of fat as you can and cut into strips about 1/2-inch wide and 2 inches long.
5. In a large skillet, heat the olive oil over high heat. Add the green pepper, garlic and tripe. Sauté for 3 minutes.
6. Add the tomatoes, mint and egg shell, bring to a boil, reduce to a simmer and cook, covered, for 30 minutes.
7. Garnish with the parmesan cheese.

Prep Time: 30 minutes
Cook Time: 2 hours
Yields: 7 – 1 cup servings
Calories: 178
Calories from fat: 88

sardine parfait

Kirby loves sardines which I sometimes chop up and add to his meal. He also loves cottage cheese. I was in a festive mood so I decided to be a little creative since I'm sure he appreciated the extra effort!

Ingredients

    2 (3.75 oz.) cans of sardines packed in oil
    2 tablespoons low fat cottage cheese
    1 peeled and finely minced pear

Directions

1. Drain the sardines and puree in a blender.
2. Scoop into center of bowl.
3. Spoon the cottage cheese around the mound of sardines.
4. Top with the pears and serve.

Why not mix it up! Pick a fave cheese. Pick a fave veggie. Pick a fave fruit. The combinations are endless ...and fun ...and healthy ...and tasty!

Prep Time: 10 minutes	Cook Time: None	
Yields: 1 serving	Calories: 650	Calories from fat: 380

savory scrambled eggs

Salty cured anchovies aren't exactly fishy. In many ways they are the aquatic version of bacon which can be shockingly intense or pungent when left whole. The texture and flavor isn't for everyone but you might be surprised at how often you eat them without knowing. Did you know the flavor in Worcestershire sauce relies hugely on the anchovy?

Scotch Woodcock is a traditional Scottish recipe from the Victorian period which was spread on toast served at the end of a meal before dessert. This is my dog friendly version of that recipe. You can serve it alone or as a topping for kibble.

Ingredients

3 large eggs
1 (2 oz.) can anchovies in light olive oil
3 tablespoons Greek yogurt with peaches
1/8 teaspoon ground egg shell

Directions

1. Whisk the eggs and chop the anchovies into small pieces.
2. Pour the oil from the can of anchovies into a non-stick sauce pan and slowly cook the eggs over low heat constantly working them with a spatula.
3. Add the anchovies and ground egg shell to the eggs when they are about halfway cooked.
4. When the eggs are done remove from the heat and stir in the yogurt.
5. Let cool and serve

I drain the anchovies (saving the olive oil) and soak them in milk for 10-15 minutes to remove much of the salt.

Prep Time: 5 minutes	Cook Time: 10 minutes	
Yields: 2 – 1/2 cup servings	Calories: 157	Calories from fat: 83

savory turkey muttloaf

This muttloaf is chock full of flavorful and beneficial seasonings. The coconut milk gives these loaves a delicious moistness and nicely balances the flavors. The first time I made these the aroma kept Kirby's attention and he was already in his expected down position before I had set his plate on the floor. I made him pose for a picture and, when I was done, he didn't even bother to get up but instead leaned his face into the plate to slurp up every bite. He then circled the plate licking every inch hoping to find a missed morsel.

Ingredients

1 lb. ground turkey
1 cup coconut milk
1 cup chopped carrots
2 cups chopped spinach
1 tablespoon coconut oil
1 teaspoon cayenne pepper
½ teaspoon garlic powder
½ teaspoon sea salt
½ teaspoon ground ginger
¼ teaspoon ground turmeric
¼ teaspoon ground cinnamon
½ teaspoon ground egg shell

Directions

1. Heat the coconut oil in a large pan. Sauté the veggies until very tender. Combine the seasonings and stir in. Remove from heat and let cool.
2. In a large bowl, add the turkey, coconut milk, and cooled veggie mixture. Thoroughly mix using your hands.
3. Evenly spoon the mixture into lightly oiled loaf tins.
4. Bake at 350 degrees for 45 minutes.
5. Remove from the oven and let rest for about 15 minutes to let the loaves firm up before removing from the tin.

You can add a cup of cooked brown rice if you need some carbohydrates.

Prep Time: 20 minutes	Cook Time: 45 minutes	
Yields: 12 mini loaves	Calories: 136 each	Calories from fat: 91 each

scrambled eggs & tuna

This recipe has come in handy a few times when we were visiting family and ran out of Kirby's food. It's quick, easy and most everyone should have these items in their refrigerator.

Ingredients

- 1 (5 oz.) can drained tuna in water
- 2 beaten large eggs
- ½ cup low fat cottage cheese
- 2 tablespoons extra light olive oil
- 1/8 teaspoon ground egg shell

Directions

1. Heat the olive oil in a small sauce pan over low heat.
2. Cook the eggs working them with a spatula.
3. Add in the tuna and cottage cheese stirring until heated through.
4. Remove pan from stove top and let cool before serving.

You can use tuna packed in oil but I prefer light olive oil or salmon oil over vegetable oils. This recipe is quite adaptable to changes - use chicken or beef in place of the tuna, use cheddar cheese or feta cheese in place of the cottage cheese. Trust me - they'll be begging for seconds!

Prep Time: 5 minutes	Cook Time: 5 minutes	
Yields: 2 servings	Calories: 333	Calories from fat: 199

Thanksgiving Dinner

thanksgiving dinner

You know that big, scrumptious dinner served every year on Thanksgiving Day? The one everyone looks forward to with salivating anticipation? The one your dog is hoping you'll share? Well, these are the next best thing without all the added ingredients your dog shouldn't be eating.

Ingredients

1 pound ground turkey
1 cup chopped sweet potato or pure pumpkin
1 cup old fashioned oats or instant mashed potato flakes
½ cup chopped green beans
1 large egg
¼ cup cranberry sauce
¼ cup apple juice
¼ teaspoon sea salt
¼ teaspoon cayenne pepper
¼ teaspoon dried rosemary
¼ teaspoon ground cinnamon
¼ teaspoon ground turmeric
¼ teaspoon dried parsley
¼ teaspoon ground egg shell

Directions

1. First choose between sweet potato or pumpkin. If you want the sweet potato then peel and mash a large cooked sweet potato.
2. Next choose between old fashioned oats or instant mashed potato flakes.
3. Chop the green beans into small pieces.
4. In a large bowl thoroughly mix together all the ingredients.
5. Evenly divide the mixture into an oiled 8 mini loaf pan or 12 cup muffin tin.
6. Bake at 350 degrees for 40 - 45 minutes.
7. Remove from the oven and let cool. They will be soft but will set as they cool.
8. Pipe or spread plain, mashed sweet potato or pure pumpkin puree on top of each loaf or muffin.

Prep Time: 10 minutes	Cook Time: 40 minutes	Yields: 12 muffines or 8 mini loaves
Potatoes & Oats	Calories: 137/206 each	Calories from fat: 49/74 each
Pumpkin & Potato Flakes	Calories: 106/160 each	Calories from fat: 42/63 each

The Fabulous Frittata

the fabulous frittata

The frittata is the Italian version of an omelet. It's a tasty way to utilize those leftovers in the refrigerator, however, for me it's not easy to prepare. Until I discovered an easy way to cook them using a spring form pan - I am so in love with the Cooking Channel!

Sometimes the occasion may call for something a little more fancy which makes a frittata the perfect choice. Either way it's an appealing, healthy and tasty meal for both the humans and the canines in your family.

Ingredients

6 large eggs
1 cup shredded cooked chicken
1 cup chopped spinach
½ cup shredded cheddar cheese
1 cup diced tomatoes
¼ cup pitted and chopped black olives
Pinch of sea salt
1/8 teaspoon ground egg shell

These happened to be the ingredients I had on hand but you can use any leftovers. The options are endless. I like them thin but if you prefer them thicker and fluffier, use ten to twelve large eggs and adjust the cooking time accordingly.

Directions

1. Preheat the oven to 400 degrees.
2. Line the bottom of your spring form pan with wax paper and place on a baking sheet to catch any leakage. Spray sides of pan with some olive oil.
3. Evenly spread all of your ingredients except the eggs.
4. Lightly whip the eggs just enough to blend (over mixing can cause them to be tough) and pour evenly over the top.
5. Immediately place in the oven and bake for about 15 minutes until golden and puffy and the center is firm and springy.

This will keep for a few days in the refrigerator but doesn't freeze well.

Prep Time: 10 minutes	Cook Time: 15 minutes	
Yields: 14 servings	Calories: 66	Calories from fat: 35

tuna salad

Tuna and veggies - just 2 ingredients, just 2 minutes, dinner is served! Kirby loves fish which is a good thing since tuna is low in fat and calories and packed with lean protein, vitamins B and D, and omega-3 fatty acids. Of course all Kirby cares about is that it tastes good.

Ingredients

1 (5 oz.) drained can tuna in water
3 heaping teaspoons natural vegetable baby food
1/8 teaspoon ground egg shell

Directions

1. Place the tuna in a small bowl.
2. Stir in the baby food.
3. Mix well and serve.

Any dog friendly veggies will work so use the ones your dog likes or, since they are pureed, now is the time to sneak in those veggies your dog doesn't particularly like. I think Kirby must be the only dog in the world who doesn't like carrots so I try to incorporate them into a lot of his meals and treats.

Choose natural baby foods containing veggies and water only. Avoid any containing sugar, seasonings, or additives.

Prep Time: 5 minutes	Cook Time: None	
Yields: 1 cup	Calories: 289	Calories from fat: 103

venison stew

If you're lucky enough to know a hunter this hearty meal has a light calorie count yet it's filling at the same time. I guarantee the aroma will lure the finickiest dog to the kitchen for a nourishing bowl. Slice up some crusty bread for the humans for a complete meal.

Ingredients

1 ½ lbs. venison, cut into 2 inch cubes
½ teaspoon sea salt
¼ teaspoon cayenne pepper
4 tablespoons flour
3 tablespoons extra light olive oil
4 to 5 chopped small potatoes
1 small chopped sweet potato
3 chopped carrots
4 chopped celery sticks
1 tablespoon unsalted butter
3 tablespoons dried parsley
1 tablespoon dried rosemary
½ teaspoon garlic powder
½ teaspoon ground egg shell
4 cups bone (beef) broth

Directions

1. Place the meat in a large bowl and, using your hands, toss it with the sea salt, cayenne pepper, and 2 tablespoons of the flour until well coated.
2. Heat a Dutch oven or pot on medium heat and brown the meat in the olive oil.
3. Whisk the remaining 2 tablespoons of flour into one cup of the bone broth and add to the pot. Add the remaining ingredients.
4. Bring to a boil and then reduce to a simmer with the lid slightly ajar for 2 to 3 hours or until the meat easily falls apart.
5. Let cool and serve.

This can easily be cooked in a crock pot. Once the meat has been browned, just throw everything in.

Prep Time: 30 minutes	Cook Time: 2-3 hours	
Yields: 11 –1 cup servings	Calories: 206	Calories from fat: 56

toppers & side dishes

If your dog eats kibble, or you want to add a little extra to their homemade meal, these are nutritious bites for a healthy dose of vitamins and minerals.

Coconut Butter	248
Kibble Gravy	249
Peanut Butter	250
Pumpkin Please	251
Roasted Baby Carrots	253
Roasted Sweet Potatoes	255
Vita Veggie Mashup	256

coconut butter

We love coconut flour and coconut oil which has just the right sweetness and is loaded with healthy benefits. Well we discovered coconut butter and love it.

Wondering what the difference is between coconut oil and coconut butter? Coconut oil is the oil extracted from the coconut where coconut butter is made from raw dried shredded coconut. When you puree the shredded coconut the coconut oil and coconut meat mix together and turn into a butter spread. To make your own use unsweetened, dried coconut, either shredded or flakes, which will turn into a somewhat smooth butter. Do not use desiccated, sweetened, reduced fat or fresh coconut. This does require a powerful food processor or blender to make.

So what can you do with coconut butter? Spoon coconut butter straight from the jar and mix in the meal time kibble, add it to baked treats, melt and pour over sweet potatoes or baked carrots, freeze for pupsicles, the list is endless. Coconut butter isn't just for dogs either! Humans can use it as a coffee creamer, a spread for toast, in curry dishes, and smoothies to name a few. Try making different flavored coconut butters: mix 1 tablespoon carob powder with 1/4 cup coconut butter, 1 tablespoon peppermint oil with 1/4 cup coconut butter, or 1 tablespoon cinnamon with 1/4 cup coconut butter.

Ingredients

2 cups unsweetened coconut, shredded or flakes

Directions

1. Place the coconut in your food processor or blender and mix on high speed scraping down the sides often for about 15 to 20 minutes or until a thick paste is formed.
   The coconut will go through three stages - first the texture will be finely shredded, then thin out into a grainy liquid, then finally turn into a somewhat smooth, thick mixture. The finished butter will seem runny but when you taste it the texture will be like a thick, slightly grainy peanut butter.
2. Pour the butter into a small glass jar with a lid and enjoy.

Store in a glass jar in the pantry for up to at least two months. Don't keep it in the refrigerator because the cold hardens it.

If it refuses to turn to butter add just the tiniest bit of coconut oil to the blender. The consistency depends on room temperature. In warm climates it is a thick liquid. In cold climates it solidifies in to a hard, wax-like substance. To bring it back to a butter consistency zap it for about 10 seconds in the microwave.

Prep Time: 15 - 20 minutes	Cook Time: None	
Yields: 1 cup	Calories: 35 per Tbsp.	Calories from fat: 30 per Tbsp.

kibble gravy

Kirby craves his dry kibble which I know is hard on a dog's digestive system causing the kidneys to work overtime. So we compromise with a small handful in the mornings if he requests it. Some days he does, some days he doesn't. I pour the kibble in one of his interactive toys if I'm headed out the door. When I have time this gravy is a quick, easy way to add flavor and additional moisture. I store it in the refrigerator in a mason jar so I can spoon out a few tablespoons into a small bowl and slightly warm in the microwave before mixing into the kibble.

This is especially popular with our foster dogs who we feed mainly kibble since we found the first few initially refused to eat kibble at their forever homes since they had become accustomed to home-made meals.

Ingredients

- 1 cup bone broth or chicken stock
- 2 tablespoons arrowroot
- 2 tablespoons cool water
- 1 teaspoon garlic powder
- 1/2 teaspoon sea salt

Directions

1. Warm the broth in a small pot over low heat.
2. Whisk together the arrowroot with the water until dissolved. Arrowroot will clump if you add it directly to the liquid you want to thicken.
3. Add the dissolved arrowroot mixture to the warm broth using a whisk.
4. Remove from the heat as soon as the broth thickens (about 30 seconds to 1 minute) because overheating will break down arrowroot's thickening properties.
5. Add in the seasonings

This can be stored in the refrigerator for up to a week.

You can also make gravy using instant mashed potato flakes in place of the arrowroot. Grind the flakes into a fine flour using a food processor or blender. Whisk in a teaspoon at a time to the warm broth until you have a gravy consistency.

Prep Time: 5 minutes	Cook Time: 1 minute	
Yields: 1 cup	Calories: 4 per tbsp.	Calories from fat: 1 per tbsp.

peanut butter

Ask any dog and they'll tell you peanut butter is at the top of their favorite flavors. The problem is not all peanut butter is created equal. Most commercially made peanut butters contain added white sugars, trans fatty acids, and aflatoxins which are considered toxic to both dogs and humans.

So what can you do? I suppose the first choice would be to eliminate all peanut butter from your dog's diet. Maybe a better option would be to limit the amount of peanut butter your dog eats and make your own fresh peanut butter. One way is to purchase raw peanuts. We usually buy 3 lb. bags of shelled, raw peanuts. I roast them on a baking sheet at 250 degrees for several hours until they are roasted to my taste. Once they have cooled I rub the skins off with my hands.

My second option in a pinch is Planter's Dry Roasted Unsalted Peanuts which have 0 trans fats because they're cooked without oil. Read the ingredient label - you're looking for peanuts, nothing else.

Ingredients

- 2 cups roasted peanuts
- 1/2 teaspoon sea salt (optional)
- 2 tablespoons honey (optional)

Directions

1. Place the peanuts in a blender or food processor and pulse a few times just until they are chopped.
2. Run the blender or food processor continuously for 1 minute. Stop and scrape down the sides and bottom of the bowl. The peanut butter will look gritty and dry at this stage.
3. Run again for another minute. Stop and scrape down the sides. The peanut butter will start clumping together.
4. Run again for another minute. Stop and scrape down the sides. The peanut butter will look glossy and soft.
5. Sprinkle the sea salt and honey over the top of the peanut butter and continue blending until it becomes completely smooth and spreadable. You can add a tablespoon or two of peanut oil if it's too thick and dry.

The peanut butter can be used immediately and will keep for several weeks in the refrigerator.

Prep Time: 5 minutes	Cook Time: None	
Yields: 1-1/2 cups	Calories: 74 per Tbsp.	Calories from fat: 54 per Tbsp.

pumpkin please

Pumpkin is considered one of the top foods for both humans and dogs for good reason. It's packed with vitamin A, potassium, and iron. It works as a remedy for both loose stools and constipation. Pumpkin is usually hard to find outside the fall months so I stock up cans of this power food while it's available. Be sure to check the expiration dates. You can use fresh pumpkin, just cook and purée. This can be served as a side dish, mixed with kibble, or frozen for those really hot dawg days of summer.

Ingredients

1 (15 oz.) can pure pumpkin
1 (13.5 oz.) can coconut milk
2 teaspoons ground cinnamon
2 teaspoons ground ginger
1 teaspoon pure vanilla extract
2 tablespoons maple syrup or honey
½ cup shredded unsweetened coconut (optional)

Directions

1. Pour the coconut milk into a medium size pot.
2. Add the cinnamon, ginger, and vanilla. Whisk to fully blend.
3. Whisk in the pumpkin. Continue to stir while cooking over low heat until warmed which will melt any fat in the coconut milk and meld all the flavors.
4. Add the maple syrup a tablespoon at a time until you have the desired sweetness. Kirby, my chief taste tester, is quite happy at two tablespoons.
5. Once heated through, pour into a bowl and let cool.

Don't use pumpkin pie filling which is loaded with ingredients your dog should not eat.

When we have fosters, I'll keep a bowl in the refrigerator to add a scoop to their meals. Otherwise I freeze it in ice cube sizes so I can grab one when I want to add it.

Prep Time: 5 minutes	Cook Time: 10 minutes	
Yields: 9 – 1/2 cup servings	Calories: 145	Calories from fat: 106

roasted baby carrots

Many dogs love to munch on a raw carrot savoring their natural sweetness. Not the Kirbster! He will take it from my hand and then immediately drop it showing no further interest. Carrots are such a healthy vegetable I wanted to find a way to entice him. I roast veggies in the oven and on the grill all the time so I thought it was worth a try. As the carrots roast, their natural sugars are released making them really sweet. Since we all know Kirby has a sweet tooth I was hoping this technique would work. And it does!

Ingredients

2 cups baby carrots
¼ cup extra light olive oil
1/8 teaspoon sea salt
1/8 teaspoon cayenne pepper

Directions

1. Slice off the tips of the carrots, cut in half lengthwise, and place in a medium bowl.
2. Add the olive oil, sea salt and cayenne pepper.
3. Use your hand to toss the carrots until they are completely coated.
4. Spread out in a single layer on a foil lined baking sheet.
5. Bake at 400 degrees for 20 to 30 minutes or until the carrots are tender-crisp and lightly browned.
6. Remove from the oven and drain the oil.
7. Let cool before serving.

The carrots will shrink while baking: 2 cups raw will yield 1 cup cooked. Kirby likes cayenne pepper but you can leave it out if your pup doesn't.

Baby carrots are actually whole carrots peeled and cut down to size. These are a great nonfat treat I like to keep in the refrigerator for about a week. I also mix in some I've shredded to his meals for a little nutritious sweetness.

Next time you fire up the grill throw some into a foil pouch to roast!

Prep Time: 10 minutes	Cook Time: 30 minutes	
Yields: 4 – ¼ cup servings	Calories: 160	Calories from fat: 127

Roasted Sweet Potatoes

roasted sweet potatoes

Kirby likes sweet potato so roasting them is a yummy way to get that naturally sweet taste. The outsides are slightly crispy with soft, tender centers. They can be seasoned to your dog's liking but I like them too with just a bit of saltiness. Delicious and healthy!

We roast them in the oven and on the grill with yummy results. They're perfect for a side dish or just as a snack which can most definitely be shared with everyone.

Ingredients

3 medium sweet potatoes
1 tablespoon extra light olive oil
1 teaspoon sea salt

Directions

1. Wash the sweet potatoes and cut into ½ inch rounds discarding the ends.
2. Place the rounds on a lined baking sheet and brush both sides with the olive oil.
3. Sprinkle the sea salt over the tops.
4. Bake at 350 degrees for 15 minutes, turn them over, and bake another 15 minutes.
5. Turn the oven up to 400 degrees and bake another 15 to 20 minutes or until they are golden brown and slightly crispy.
6. Let cool and serve slightly warm.

Prep Time: 10 minutes	Cook Time: 30 minutes
Yields: 24 slices	Calories: 27 each Calories from fat: 6 each

vita veggie mashup

Some dogs love their veggies, others not so much. Kirby, like many children, doesn't particularly like veggies so I sneak them in his food by finely chopping or pureeing them. He may be the only dog who refuses a raw carrot or green bean!

This mashup is chock full of vitamins and minerals. It can be adjusted to your dog's preference or dietary needs by choosing any dog friendly vegetables. Add some fruit for a little sweetness.

Ingredients

2 large chopped green peppers
1 peeled chopped cucumber
1 large bunch kale, stems removed
1 (12 oz.) bag butternut squash
1 (12 oz.) bag broccoli & cauliflower
1 (12 oz.) bag green beans

Directions

1. Puree the green peppers and cucumber in a food processor or blender. Pour into a large bowl.
2. Lightly cook the remaining produce in a large pot until tender.
3. Strain and puree in a food processor or blender. Pour into the bowl and stir until thoroughly mixed.

This can be stored in the refrigerator for up to a week or in the freezer up to three months. I like to freeze it in small silicone molds, or ice cube trays, and then place in a freezer safe zip lock bag. Take out what you need, let thaw, and stir into your dog's meal or pour over kibble. It can also be served by itself as a cool drink or warm soup.

Prep Time: 20 minutes	Cook Time: 20 minutes	
Yields: 7 cups (48 cubes)	Calories: 77	Calories from fat: 2

make your own chicken stock

Most store brands contain onion powder, etc. which are harmful for dogs. The only truly natural brand I have found is Swanson Flavor Boost which doesn't contain any added ingredients - no artificial flavors, colors, preservatives, MSG, or most importantly onion. I use it in a pinch but usually I find that it's easy and much cheaper to make it myself.

Whenever I cook a chicken (boiled, baked, grilled), or buy a rotisserie chicken, I save the skin and bones for the stock, including leftover meat from the dinner plates. I also use the gizzard, heart and neck if available. I throw everything in a large freezer bag which I store in my freezer until I'm ready to cook up a batch.

Ingredients

1 Chicken carcass
Chicken feet (optional)
Veggies (optional)
Seasonings (optional)

Directions:

1. Place leftover chicken bones and skin in a Dutch oven or large pot and cover with water. Add a few chicken feet for gelatin. Most often I make pure chicken stock so I can add what I want when making a certain dish but you can add any chopped veggies or seasonings that are safe for dogs when you make your stock.
2. Simmer on low heat letting some of the water boil off for at least 4-5 hours. Leave the pot covered but slightly ajar until the last half hour or so.
3. Strain the stock through a small mesh colander. The fat will rise to the top and harden so just skim it off before using. It can be stored in the refrigerator up to 48 hours but any longer and it should be frozen.

Even easier is using your crock pot. Cover the bones and skin with cold water. Start on highest setting and bring to a boil. Then slow cook for at least five hours on high or overnight on low.

I like to freeze the stock in silicone molds or ice cube trays. Once frozen, I pop them out and place in zip lock freezer bags with the date written on the bag. Each cube contains 2 tablespoons or 1 ounce. 12 ice cubes equal roughly 1 cup. Whenever I need some chicken stock for a meal, human or canine, or some treats I just grab a few cubes from the freezer and I'm good to go!

Prep Time: 20 minutes	Cook Time: 4-5 hours

make your own bone broth

Bone (beef) broth is a powerful health tonic rich in nutrients and minerals, a rich source of gelatin and glucosamine chondroitin. In fact, many people consume it daily believing it contributes to maintaining a healthy body. In times of illness it supports the body but is very easy to digest so the body's energy can focus on healing. Homemade broth is always richer and more flavorful than the store varieties which almost always contain ingredients deemed dangerous for dogs.

Try to use several types of bones. Grass-fed beef is best but don't worry if you can't find any. If you don't have a local butcher, as a last resort, use meaty beef neck bones which can normally be found at your local grocery store. The important steps are roasting the meaty bones to caramelize the flavors and adding the vinegar which draws the minerals out of the bones. You can also roast the vegetables too.

If you don't like the flavor of your broth, just simmer it longer, maybe leaving the lid off if it's too pale. Once it reduces, you can see what the flavor is really like. Adding veggies and seasonings will bring out the flavors.

Ingredients

- 2 lbs. of beef marrow and knuckle bones
- 1 lb. meaty rib or neck bones
- 3 quarts cold filtered water
- 1/3 cup apple cider vinegar
- 3 chopped carrots (optional)
- 3 chopped celery sticks (optional)
- 1 bunch of fresh parsley
- 1 tablespoon sea salt
- 2 crushed cloves of garlic or 1 teaspoon garlic powder

Directions

1. Place the bones that have meaty bits on them in a roasting pan and brown in the oven at 350 degrees until well-browned (60 minutes). Turn over after 30 minutes.
2. Place all of your non-meaty marrow bones in a large pot, add the water, vinegar and optional vegetables. Let sit while the meaty bones are browning.
3. Add the browned bones to the pot, deglaze the roasting pan with hot water and get up all of the brown bits and pour this liquid into the pot. Add additional water if needed to cover the bones.
4. Bring to a boil and remove the scum/foam that rises to the top. You don't need to remove any floating fat. Reduce heat, cover and simmer for at least 12 hours and as long as 72 hours. The longer you cook the stock, the more rich and flavorful it will be.

5. After several hours you will want to remove any of the meat or marrow you need for other recipes.
6. Simmer for 12-48 hours. Add more water when needed to keep the bones covered.
7. During the last 30 minutes, add the parsley, sea salt and garlic.
8. Remove the bones and strain the stock.

Store in wide mouth mason jars leaving an inch head room from the top of the stock to the top of the jar so as the stock freezes and expands it won't break the glass. Let the jars cool, then freeze or refrigerate. You can remove the congealed fat after refrigerating or even freezing. I also freeze enough in ice cube trays to fill a large zip lock bag for quick additions to Kirby's meals or to use in recipes where I don't need very much.

This is my basic recipe but now and then I'll add some fresh spinach, broccoli, asparagus, peas, kale, or green beans to the mason jars just for the dogs.

Crock Pot Method

Make sure to use both roasted meaty and non meaty bones.

1. Use the biggest crock pot you have. I have an 8 1/2 quart crock pot and use about 3 pounds of bones.
2. Don't overfill with water since it won't evaporate as quickly as with a stockpot. Make sure the lid is weighted down and that simmering can't move the lid around or you will have water everywhere.
3. Put on high until it gets going then turn down to low.
4. Skim the scum/foam that rises to the top as needed.
5. Cook for 24 to 48 hours.

Tip: Label large zip lock bags and over time just throw leftover bones and vegetable scraps in the freezer.

the

pantry

tips & tricks

This journey into canine cuisine has been a learn as I go journey so this will help clarify how I prepare or use certain ingredients, basically those little tips and tricks I've learned over the years to use in my kitchen.

Adding Water
When cooking a soup or stew and you find you need to add more water during the cooking process, use hot water since adding cold water will slow down the whole cooking process.

Cooking Bacon in the Oven
Preheat the oven to 400°F with a rack in center of the oven. Arrange the bacon close together even slightly overlapping in a single layer on a foil lined baking sheet which makes clean-up easier. Bake for 15 to 18 minutes or until the bacon is deep golden-brown and crispy. Exact baking time will depend on the thickness of the bacon and how crispy you like it. Begin checking around 12 minutes to monitor how quickly the bacon is cooking. Once cooked remove the bacon from the oven and use tongs to transfer it to a paper towel lined plate to drain and finish crisping. Cooked bacon can be kept in an air tight container in the refrigerator for up to a week or in the freezer for up to three months.

Cutting Meat
Cutting or slicing meat to grind or cook can be tricky even with a sharp knife. To make it easier, place the meat in the freezer for 10 to 15 minutes to stiffen it up.

Flax Seed
Whole flax seed will stay fresh for up to a year if stored correctly. Purchase from a source where you're sure there is rapid turnover. Ideally it should be refrigerated at the store. The bag should be opaque since light will accelerate the meal going rancid. Vacuum-packed packaging is the best because it prevents the meal from having contact with oxygen before opening.

Whole flax seed should be stored in a cool, dark, dry place preferably in the refrigerator or freezer to be on the safe side. Flax meal should be stored in the freezer and used up within a few weeks. Since flax seed will go rancid more quickly after being ground into meal it's safer to buy whole flax seed and grind it yourself in a coffee grinder (set aside one that is NOT used to grind coffee beans which are toxic to dogs). It should have a mildly nutty taste so if it is at all bitter, throw it away. A 3/4 cup of whole flax seed yields 1 cup of flax meal.

Honey
Many recipes you already use can be adjusted for your dog by omitting or replacing ingredients that aren't dog friendly. One replacement for sugar is natural honey. Because of its high fructose content, honey has a higher sweetening power than sugar. This means you can use less honey than sugar to achieve the desired sweetness. A trick is to coat the measuring cup with non-stick cooking spray or oil before adding the honey so it will slide right out. A 12-ounce jar of honey equals 1 cup.

Making Oat Flour
You can always buy oat flour in the grocery store. However, for a cheaper and healthier version make your own using old fashioned rolled oats. Blend or process on low speed in 30-second increments stirring to remove any oats that may stick to the sides or bottom of the container. Continue blending or processing until the oats are the same consistency as flour. Once ground the oats can become rancid more quickly so only grind what you're going to use. You can store any extra in an airtight container in the refrigerator for up to one month. Steel cut oats can be ground but will result in a coarser flour. 1 ¼ cups rolled oats yields 1 cup oat flour.

Making Potato Flour
Potato flour which is ground from peeled, dried potatoes provides a soft, moist texture, makes dough easier to shape and handle and increases its shelf life. Add potato flour to the dry ingredients in your recipe and whisk together before adding directly to liquid or it can clump and make lumps. You can grind instant mashed potato flakes to make your own potato flour in a food processor or blender. Read the ingredients in order to choose an all natural brand to avoid extra additives your dog doesn't need. 2 cups ground potato flakes yields 1 cup potato flour. 1/3 cup potato flakes = 1 medium potato

Removing Toxins from Liver
To release any toxins that were stored in the liver and remove some of the pungent smell, place the thawed and drained liver in a covered container with about 2 tablespoons of apple cider vinegar and refrigerate overnight.

Shipping Treats
Treats that have a crunchy or hard texture make excellent choices for mail delivery. They tend to be fairly sturdy so you don't have to worry too much about breakage and since they already have a fairly dry texture, drying out isn't much of an issue.

The trick to shipping treats is to pack them snugly in an airtight container. They should be well packed in an inner box (I like to layer the treats between paper inside the container), then well packed in a second outer box. Choose a box that is appropriate in size to the airtight container you are using. This will help keep the container from shifting and the treats from breaking. The ideal cushion is 2 to 3 inches of packing material on all sides. Use packing peanuts or Bubble Wrap to reduce rattling and any breakage. Used wrapping paper can be shredded and used for lining the boxes.

Shredding Chicken Meat
There are two ways to shred your chicken meat. Use two forks to pull the meat apart or place the cooked, skinned, and deboned chicken into the bowl of your KitchenAid Mixer. Using the paddle attachment, mix the chicken on medium speed for 20-30 seconds until it's shredded.

Storing Bananas
Most recipes require ripe bananas but there are times I have really ripe bananas sitting on my counter when I'm not ready to use them. I freeze them, sliced or still in the peel, for several months by placing them in freezer bags.

Storing Treats

First make sure they are completely cooled, otherwise they'll steam, soften up, and stick to each other. Treats can usually be stored at room temperature in airtight containers for up to a week. Appropriate containers can be cookie jars or tins, screw top jars, snap-top plastic boxes, or tightly closed zip lock bags. If you plan to store treats for more than a week then it's better to freeze them for up to 3 months.

Use a Straw

I store a lot of Kirby's treats in zip lock bags. I can write the name and date on the front and they don't take up much room in the freezer. However, all that air in there can cause ice crystals to form which in turn affects the food. That's why I use a straw! Slide the end of a straw into the baggie and zip shut as close as possible. Suck out the air, carefully remove the straw, and zip the rest of the way shut. Not as good as a machine but close enough. (I now own a Food Saver which I highly recommend.)

Vegetables - Cutting Wobbly Ones

To safely cut wobbly vegetables like potatoes, squash, and beets with a sharp knife, cut a thin slice along the length of the vegetable to create a flat side. Then turn the vegetable cut-side down on the cutting board. This will make it stable so it won't wobble. Slice until it becomes unsteady and hard to grip. Then turn the vegetable so that the broad, flat side from which you made the last cut is face down on the cutting board and finish slicing.

dealing with dough

Dough is defined as a mixture of flour, liquid and other ingredients (often including a leavening) that is stiff but pliable enough to work with the hands. Unlike a batter, dough is too stiff to pour. This cornerstone of dog treats can be made with various flours depending on your choice of grain or grain free due to allergies, dietary restrictions, or simply flavor.

Dog treats are the easiest to bake for the simple reason your dog isn't going to care what they look like - that's a human thing! These are some of the tricks and tips I use when dealing with dough.

Mixing
I almost always use my KitchenAid mixer but if you don't have one, whisk together the dry ingredients, and then add them to the wet ones, stirring until the mixture is evenly combined.

Chilling
After mixing my dough, I like to set the covered bowl in the refrigerator to let it chill which firms up the fat giving the flour time to absorb the liquid evenly. This makes the dough much less sticky, roll out more evenly, and hold its shape while being cut and transferred to a baking sheet.

Rolling
I adore my Silpat Roller and non-stick mat since nothing is sticking to those babies! Before I would place the dough on a lightly floured surface, place a sheet of parchment paper on top of the dough, and then roll. I would also use the same paper as the liner on my baking sheet.

Another trick I've learned is to place the dough inside a large zip lock bag, roll it to the thickness you want, then cut open the sides, remove the top, and use your cookie cutters right on the bag. No flour needed.

Scooping
(1) Fill a spoon halfway with the dough. Using another spoon of the same size, scrape the dough off the first spoon onto the baking sheet.

(2) I like using my cookie scoops. I have two metal ones (1/2 inch and 1 inch) and a silicone one with a rubber top I can press to release sticky dough. Scoop the dough against the side of the bowl using the lip of the bowl to level off the bottom then release the dough. This results in a more consistent size.

Freezing
Most of my recipes make way more than Kirby can eat before they spoil which means I often freeze the baked treats (quite a bit gets delivered to the shelter) or the uncooked dough for later. Dough can be frozen for up to three months. There are several ways to do this just be sure to label the name of the treat and the date made.

The method I prefer is to place the dough in a large zip lock freezer bag and roll it out like a pie crust. When ready to use, let thaw, roll out to desired thickness, and cut out the cookies with cookie cutters.

Another way is to form the dough into logs for slice-and-bake cookies. Form the dough into a log with the help of parchment paper or waxed paper and store the logs in a large zip-lock freezer bag. Don't thaw the dough before baking, use a sharp knife to cut as few or as many as you want, place them on a parchment lined baking sheet, and let them thaw while the oven is heating up.

A final trick is to prepare your balled or drop cookies up until the point of baking them, freeze them on a baking sheet, and then place in zip-lock freezer bags. This way you can get as few or as many as you want out of the freezer and let them thaw on the cookie sheet while your oven is heating up.

Use a drinking straw to suck the air out of the bags before closing.

is it still good?

Most produce at the grocery store has traveled a long way to land in the bins. That's why they are usually sprayed with gas to enhance the color, waxed to look shiny, and treated to last awhile on store shelves. So natural isn't always completely natural. Please don't think I'm trying to deter you from the produce section. I use a lot of these fresh ingredients. I just want you to be aware that canned and frozen are more than suitable for healthy consumption.

For the freshest fruits and vegetables grow your own or opt for a farmer's market if you are lucky enough to have one nearby. If I'm not planning to use the produce right away I usually freeze it. I like to chop and blanche the vegetables. I peel and chop fruits before freezing them. Berries are delicate so I freeze them without rinsing. Washington's Green Grocer is a great online source of information for storing fresh I use all the time that covers, as far as I can tell, every fruit and vegetable there is.

Did you know that sometimes canned or frozen fruits and vegetables are more nutritious than fresh? That's because the longer fruits and vegetables sit in the grocery store, the more nutrients they are losing. But fruits and vegetables grown for freezing or canning are usually processed by the manufacturer's right after they're picked. Therefore, they retain more nutrients.

Pay Attention to Expiration Dates

Fruits and vegetables are seasonal which makes canned or frozen fruits and vegetables even more convenient since you can stock up on the ingredients you use the most especially when you catch a sale. The trick is understanding the expiration dates which usually aren't safety dates at all.

Use By, Best if Used By, Best By, and Best Before dates are generally found on shelf-stable products like peanut butter and honey. These dates are voluntarily provided by the manufacturer to let you know how long the product is likely to remain at its absolute best quality when unopened. After that date has passed, you may start to notice gradual changes in the product's texture, color, or flavor but as long as you've been storing the item properly you can generally consume it beyond this date. To decide whether a product with this type of date is still of satisfactory quality is to smell and taste it first. Always discard foods that have developed an off odor, flavor or appearance.

Sell By dates are found on perishable items like meat, seafood, poultry and milk. This date is a guide for stores to know how long they can display a particular product. Some claim you can still store it at home for some time beyond that date as long as you follow safe storage procedures

Expires On dates are usually only on infant formula and some baby foods which are the only food products the federal government regulates with regard to dating. You should always use the product before this expiration date has passed.

A good tip I follow is to copy the grocery stores when storing items in your pantry or freezer by always moving the older items forward and storing the newer items behind. I'm unbelievable picky about sandwich bread so I always reach for the loaf in the back near the bottom with the farthest use by date.

stocking the pantry

This is the list of staples I try to keep on hand for Kirby's meals and treats which are ongoing endeavors in order to provide him with a long, healthy, vibrant life.

Dry Goods
Applesauce, natural
Baking Powder & Soda
Blackstrap Molasses
Canned Beans (black, garbanzo, lentils)
Canned Fish (anchovies, mackerel, salmon, sardines, tuna)
Canned Pure Pumpkin
Carob (chips, powder)
Coconut, shredded
Dried Fruit
Flours (barley, brown rice, coconut)
Gelatin
Grains (barley, old fashioned oats)
Honey, local
Milk (almond, coconut, dry, 2%)
Natural Baby Food
Natural Peanut Butter
Oils (coconut, olive, safflower, salmon)
Pasta
Plain Bread Crumbs
Quinoa

Refrigerator
Bacon (turkey, ham)
Cheese (cheddar, feta, and parmesan)
Eggs
Plain Greek Yogurt
Pure Maple Syrup

Seasonings/Herbs
Anise (oil, seed)
Cayenne Pepper
Garlic (fresh, minced, powder)
Dried Basil
Dried Bay Leaves
Dried Lavender
Dried Mint
Dried Parsley
Dried Rosemary
Pure Vanilla Extract
Sea Salt
Ground Ceylon Cinnamon
Ground Ginger
Ground Oregano
Ground Thyme
Ground Turmeric
Whole Flax Seed

Freezer
Assorted Vegetables & Fruits
Beef
Bison
Bone Broth
Bones & carcasses for broth/stock
Chicken (whole, breasts, thighs, legs)
Chicken Stock
Fish (Tilapia, Catfish, Cod)
Organ Meats (heart, liver, gizzards)
Turkey
Venison

My Herb Garden: Basil, Parsley, Lavender, Mint, Oregano, Thyme, Rosemary.

tools in the kitchen

These are the tools and workhorses that help me create delicious, healthy dog treats and meals. You can use all of them or just a few.

Baker's Rack Allows air to circulate so freshly baked treats cool evenly and stay crisp.

Baking Pans I recommend commercial quality sheet pans which, although more expensive, are worth the investment in the long run. Choose heavy pans avoiding non-stick and dark coated pans which tend to bake too fast. I use baking sheets and muffin tins on a regular basis.

Cookie Cutters There is a plethora of cookie cutters from small to large, plastic and metal, the usual and the unusual. Metal cookie cutters should be gently hand washed and then quickly dried to prevent rust. To ensure that all nooks and crannies are dry, place the cookie cutters on a clean baking sheet in a warm, turned-off oven for a few minutes. A toaster oven may be used as well.

Colander or Fine Mesh Strainer Necessary for rinsing grains, veggies, meats, and, well, straining things!

Crockpot Great for making stews and soups because they do all the work for you. Just chop and season, then turn it on and walk away without worrying if it will burn on the bottom.

Cutting Boards Plastic ones in a multitude of colors are very popular but I much prefer wood. It's kinder to knives and won't dull them as quickly as plastic. Oiling your wooden cutting boards regularly with a food-safe oil to protect them from staining and warping will help them last for years. It's safest to designate one board for meats and one board for fruits and vegetables to avoid cross-contamination.

Dutch Oven A heavy metal pot with lid made of cast iron covered in enamel. These are great for really melding together the flavors. I probably use mine twice a month.

Food Dehydrator This is a workhorse in my kitchen! Kirby starts drooling when I get it out knowing there is bound to be some tasty jerky in his near future. It takes hours to dehydrate but the comfort from knowing he won't be chewing on a possibly tainted chew is well worth the wait not to mention it's easier on the budget.

Food Saver A great way to preserve treats in the freezer avoiding freezer burn and ice crystals. You don't need one with all the bells and whistles.

Food Chopper I use this all the time to chop, grind, and mince. It's faster than using a knife and probably saves me from losing many fingers! I have the Ninja Express Chopper and love the double blades because they chop the veggies as small as I want short of a puree unless that's what I want.

Garlic Press I add minced garlic to some of Kirby's meals so I love this tool. Mine has small silicone points that push the garlic through the holes.

Herb Shears 5 stainless steel blades (10 in all) make chopping and mincing fresh herbs a breeze! I like to cut my herbs into a small bowl, then keep cutting them with the end of the scissors until the herbs are minced to my liking. I use a flat knife to slide out the pieces caught between the blades. So much easier than using a cutting board and knife and easier clean-up than my electric chopper.

Measuring Spoons Make sure the spoons are clearly marked so you don't confuse a teaspoon with a tablespoon!

Measuring Cups for dry ingredients Standard cup sizes for dry measurements include 1/4, 1/3, 1/2, 2/3, 3/4 and 1 cup sizes. Look for measuring cups with long handles and wide, shallow bodies.

Measuring Cups for liquid ingredients Make sure there's a spout for pouring, clear measurement markings, and a sturdy handle. I have a 2 cup and a 4 cup.

Mixing Bowls There's a size for everyone and everything. I prefer ceramic since they are non-porous. Stainless steel would work as well.

Oil Mister I use this to spray my pans and baking sheets, and some foods with a fine mist of pure olive oil. It's ideal for low-fat cooking giving me control over the amount of oil used and eliminating the unhealthy additives found in products like Pam. Did you know you can quickly dry your nail polish with Pam? Makes me wonder what it can do to the body.

Parchment Paper If you don't want to invest in silicone baking mats this paper creates a disposable non-stick surface which is great for baking treats.

Silicone Baking Mats These non-stick baking sheets can be washed and used again and again.

Silicone Molds I love using these for baking pupcakes to freezing cold treats. There are so many fun shapes and sizes to choose from and cleanup is a breeze.

Stainless Steel Soap I keep one by my kitchen sink to remove odors from handling fish, onion, and garlic. I don't know how it works, it just works.

Stand Mixer This is another of my workhorses. I was fortunate to inherit my Dad's commercial 5 quart KitchenAid mixer. If, like me, you can't afford one then consider purchasing a used one. It's an investment you'll never regret.

Vegetable Peeler Indispensable when it comes to preparing healthy, fresh veggies.

Wax Paper A necessity when dehydrating meats to save on clean-up time.

Ziploc Containers with lids These are inexpensive and re-usable. I freeze Kirby's meals in the one cup size.

conversion charts

Herb/Spice	Dried Measurement	Fresh Amount
Basil	1 teaspoon	2 teaspoons
Bay Leaf	2 leaves	1 leaf
Dill	1 teaspoon	3 teaspoons
Garlic	1/8 teaspoon ground	1 clove
Ginger	¼ teaspoon ground	1 teaspoon
Parsley	1 teaspoon	2 teaspoons
Mint	1 teaspoon	2 teaspoons
Thyme	¾ teaspoon ground	1 tablespoon
Rosemary	1 teaspoon	1 tablespoon

U.S. Volume	Metric Volume
¼ teaspoon	1.23 ml
½ teaspoon	2.5 ml
¾ teaspoon	3.7 ml
1 teaspoon	4.9 ml
1 ½ teaspoons / ½ tablespoon	7.5 ml
2 teaspoons	10 ml
3 teaspoons / 1 tablespoon	15 ml
1/8 cup / 2 tablespoons / 1 ounce	30 ml
¼ cup / 4 tablespoons / 2 ounces	60 ml
½ cup / 8 tablespoons / 4 ounces	120 ml
¾ cup / 12 tablespoons / 6 ounces	180 ml
1 cup / 16 tablespoons / 8 ounces	240 ml

Oven Temperatures

Fahrenheit	Celsius
200 degrees F	93 degrees C
250 degrees F	130 degrees C
275 degrees F	140 degrees C
300 degrees F	150 degrees C
325 degrees F	165 degrees C
350 degrees F	177 degrees C
375 degrees F	190 degrees C
400 degrees F	200 degrees C

Bath Time

the soap of royalty dog shampoo

Now that you're taking care of the inside, here's a safe shampoo for the outside. Kirby gets a bath every week with dirty paws or muzzle washed in the kitchen sink when needed. Most commercial dog shampoos have dangerous chemicals I don't care to have his skin absorb: Sodium Laureth Sulfate, Sodium Lauryl ether Sulfate, Synthetic Fragrances, BHA (butylated hydroxyanisole), Diaminobenzene, Methylisothiazolinone, Dioxins, Artificial colors, Benzalkonium, Chloride, Benzethonium Chloride, Diethanolamine, Methicone, Triethanolamine, Propylene Glycol, Petrolatum, Mineral Oil, and Sodium Hydroxide.

If you search you can find natural dog shampoos but they can be expensive. I've been using Kirk's Original Coco Castile Soap which has been around since 1839 to make Kirby's shampoo, dish soap, dishwasher detergent, soap dispenser refill, body wash, and a veggie wash. The ingredients are coconut soap, water, vegetable glycerin, coconut oil, and natural fragrance. There's also an unscented version. This soap is made from 100% plant oils and is hypoallergenic and biodegradable with no harsh or dangerous chemicals, no animal by-product, no synthetic detergents, and never tested on animals.

"Castile" originally referred to the highly-prized vegetable based soap produced in Castile, Spain. For centuries this soap was considered "the soap of royalty" because of its luxurious lather and gentleness to the skin. Today, "Castile" refers to any vegetable based soap. So a pack of three bars for $3.28 at Wal-Mart means Kirby gets treated like royalty on a budget.

Ingredients

   2 (4 oz.) bars castile soap
   6 cups boiling water

Directions

1. Use a kitchen knife to cut the bar of soap into small slivers. This soap is so soft it's easier than slicing cheese.
2. In a medium pot heat water to boiling and then remove from heat.
3. Add the slivers of soap and leave for about an hour which will allow the soap to dissolve into a concentrated liquid.
4. Pour the liquid soap into your chosen containers.

Yields: 6 Cups

This is the ratio I like best but you can always dilute it with water either when making it or after. Coconut oil liquefies when it reaches 76 degrees so it's easy to place the container in hot water when I want the liquid form if it has become a semi-solid soap.

The more concentrated it is the more sudsy bubbles will be achieved. I use the concentrated for Kirby's baths which goes a long ways. It lathers up which I love while I massage it throughout his coat which he loves and it rinses out beautifully. The coconut smell is wonderful by itself however you can add about ¼ teaspoon or 3-5 drops of an essential oil or extract like peppermint, lavender, orange, or rosemary. My favorite is adding ¼ teaspoon pure peppermint extract from my pantry. I haven't found that this mixture irritates the eyes or mouths of Kirby or our fosters. Make sure whatever scent you choose is dog friendly, for example, tea tree oil is not.

Tip: We save those 16 oz. plastic Coffee Mate bottles, remove the labels and wash them, then fill with this shampoo for the local shelters. I use a Sharpie permanent marker to write the ingredients on the bottle which is important for dogs with sensitive skin especially if I've added any oils for aroma.

resources

I've been doing a lot of research over the years to determine the healthiest, safest ways to raise Kirby, and our fosters, to ensure vital longevity. These are the resources I turn to time and again.

Books/Journals
Dr. Pitcairn's Complete Guide to Natural Health for Dogs and Cats
The Whole Dog Journal

Reference Websites
www.dogaware.com
www.dogfoodadvisor.com
www.dogsnaturallymagazine.com
www.earthclinic.com
www,healthypets.mercola.com
www.holisticdog.org/
www.natural-dog-health-remedies.com
www.ottawavalleydogwhisperer.blogspot.com
www.petmd.com
www.raisinghealthydogs.com
www.thehonestkitchen.com

ingredient index

Almond Milk
 breakfast porridge, 185
 cheesy mashed taters, 109
 healthy ingredients, 17
 peanut butter & jelly sandwiches, 114
 secret spinach smoothies, 138

Almonds
 christmas carob bark, 123
 grrreat granola bars, 75

Anchovies
 healthy ingredients, 17
 hunter's chicken stew, 225
 savory scrambled eggs, 236

Anise
 chai chicken strips, 162
 safe herbs & spices, 29

Apples
 all american apple pie, 103
 healthy ingredients, 17
 hearty beef stew, 224

Apple Cider or Juice
 all american apple pie, 103
 thanksgiving dinner, 241

Applesauce
 bacon, eggs & quinoa, 210
 banana carob pupcakes, 54
 barkin bacon bites, 56
 b'oat bites, 58
 butternut bliss biscuits, 60
 coconut ice cream, 145
 did you say bacon? pupsicles, 148
 pawsome pumpkin pupcakes, 85
 pesto puppers, 87
 pumpkin cran muffins, 91
 sweet potato puffs, 94
 the kirbylicious barkday cake, 98

Arrowroot
 kibble gravy, 249

Asparagus
 monster mashed muttins, 230

Avocado
 avocado egg salad, 209
 carob avocado frosting, 119
 healthy ingredients, 17

Baby Food, Natural
 arroz con pollo, 181
 chazuke, 186
 chicken n greens, 216
 monster mashed muttins, 230
 muttloaf, 199
 tuna salad, 244

Bacon (ham, turkey)
 bacon, eggs & quinoa, 210
 barkin bacon bites, 56
 cajun bacon biscuits, 61
 cheesy mashed taters, 109
 chicken cordon bleu, 69
 did you say bacon? Pupsicles, 148
 healthy ingredients, 17
 liver dumplings, 227
 pumpkin cream cheese frosting, 118
 tasty tuna treats, 95

the carnivore's cake, 203
tips & tricks, 263

Baking Powder/Soda
banana carob pupcakes, 54
blueberry pupcakes, 57
carrot pupcakes, 63
harmful ingredients, 25
pawsome pumpkin pupcakes, 85
pesto puppers, 87
pumpkin cran muffins, 91
puppermint patties, 92
the kirbylicious barkday cake, 98
tips & tricks, 264

Bananas
banana carob frosting, 119
banana carob pupcakes, 54
banana lemon gummy paws, 124
banana maple crisps, 105
bananaramas, 55
b'oat bites, 58
cherry fruit leather, 163
cinnamon carob ice cream, 143
healthy ingredients, 17
power punch, 135
secret spinach smoothies, 138
sweet potato puffs, 94
tasty tuna treats, 95
tips & tricks, 264

Barbecue Sauce (plain)
hawaiian burgers, 223

Barley
chicken barley soup, 187
chicken gizzard casserole, 188
chicken gumbo, 189
healthy ingredients, 17
soak those grains, 43
southwestern chicken chili, 202

Barley Flour
liver pate' bites, 81
safe flours, 35

Basil
basil pesto, 88, 87
chicken barley soup, 187
country roots beef stew, 222
safe herbs & spices, 29

Bay Leaves
cinnamon beef stew, 219
hunter's chicken stew, 225

Beef Filet
the carnivore's cake, 203

Beef Heart
beef heart soup, 211
my sweetheart jerky, 172

Beef, Ground
beefy kale pasta, 183
cheeseburgers, 65
cottage cheese muttins, 191
hamburger helper canine style, 195
healthy ingredients, 18
liver dumplings, 227
meaty muffins, 198
monster mashed muttins, 230
muttloaf, 199
shepherd's pie, 201
twice as good beef jerky, 177

Beef Stew Meat
cinnamon beef stew, 219
country roots beef stew, 222
hearty beef stew, 224
savory beef bits, 115

Bison, Ground
bison jerky, 159

healthy ingredients, 18

Black Beans
hamburger helper canine style, 195
healthy ingredients, 18
southwestern chicken chili, 202

Black Olives
hunter's chicken stew, 225
the fabulous frittata, 243

Blueberries
blueberry chia seed jelly, 114
blueberry pupcakes, 57
chicken gumbo, 189
healthy ingredients, 18
meaty muffins, 198
patriotic pupsicles, 151
power punch, 135
viva la venison, 205

Bones (marrow, knuckle, rib, neck)
Healthy ingredients, 25
make your own bone broth, 258

Bone Broth
bark beer, 132
cheeseburgers, 65
cinnamon beef stew, 219
hearty beef stew, 224
kibble gravy, 249
liver dumplings, 227
liver pate' bites, 81
meaty gummy paws, 124
mighty dog mutt balls, 127
milk bones, 83
the big bonesicle, 153
venison stew, 245

Bread Crumbs
green eggs & ham, 75

little Italy meatballs, 197
shepherd's pie, 201
turkey burgers, 204

Broccoli
Harmful ingredients, 25
hearty beef stew, 224
vita veggie mashup, 256

Broccoli Slaw
canned fish stew, 213
coconut fish soup, 221
turkey burgers, 204

Brown Rice
arroz con pollo, 181
cinnamon beef stew, 219
cottage cheese muttins, 191
hamburger helper canine style, 195
healthy ingredients, 18
meaty muffins, 198

Brown Rice Baby Cereal
greek lamb patties, 193

Brown Rice Flour
all american apple pie, 103
bananaramas, 55
barkin bacon bites, 56
coconut catters, 70
ezy cheesy, 71
liver lover's meaty bones, 79
pb pill pockets, 129
safe flours, 35
the great plumpkin, 97

Buckwheat Flour
healthy ingredients, 18
peanut butter & jelly sandwiches, 114
safe flours, 36

Butter
- cheese nips kinda, 67
- healthy ingredients, 18
- mashed potato frosting, 120
- pb scrambled eggs, 231
- venison stew, 245

Carob (chips, powder, molasses)
- banana carob frosting, 119
- banana carob pupcakes, 54
- carob avocado frosting, 119
- carob, peanut butter, yogurt chips, 117
- christmas carob bark, 123
- cinnamon carob ice cream, 143
- healthy ingredients, 19
- peanut butter cups, 131

Carrots
- beef heart soup, 211
- carrot pupcakes, 63
- chicken barley soup, 187
- cinnamon beef stew, 219
- country roots beef stew, 222
- healthy ingredients, 19
- hearty beef stew, 224
- hunter's chicken stew, 225
- make your own bone broth, 258
- meaty muffins, 198
- monster mashed muttins, 230
- roasted baby carrots, 253
- savory turkey muttloaf, 237
- shepherd's pie, 201
- venison stew, 245

Catfish
- asian fish balls, 208
- coconut fish soup, 221

Cauliflower
- vita veggie mashup, 256

Cayenne Pepper
- asian fish balls, 208
- avocado egg salad, 209
- beef heart soup, 211
- beefy kale pasta, 183
- breakfast muffins, 212
- cheeseburgers, 65
- chicken barley soup, 187
- chicken cordon bleu, 69
- chicken gumbo, 189
- chicken liver meatballs, 215
- chicken n greens, 216
- hamburger helper canine style, 195
- hawaiian burgers, 223
- hearty beef stew, 224
- hunter's chicken stew, 225
- liver dumplings, 227
- loaves of lamb, 229
- my sweetheart jerky, 172
- oh my deer jerky, 173
- polpette di sarde, 233
- roasted baby carrots, 253
- safe herbs & spices, 30
- savory turkey muttloaf, 237
- shepherd's pie, 201
- southwestern chicken chili, 202
- thanksgiving dinner, 241
- the great plumpkin, 97
- venison stew, 245
- viva la venison, 205

Celery
- beef heart soup, 211
- chicken barley soup, 187
- make your own bone broth, 258
- venison stew, 245

Cheese, Cheddar
- breakfast muffins, 212
- cheeseburgers, 65
- cheese nips kinda, 67
- cheesy mashed taters, 109
- ezy cheesy, 71
- green eggs & ham, 75

hamburger helper canine style, 195
healthy ingredients, 19
liver lover's meaty bones, 79
shepherd's pie, 201
the fabulous frittata, 243

Cheese, Cottage
sardine parfait, 235
scrambled eggs & tuna, 239

Cheese, Cream
bacon cream cheese frosting, 118
cream cheese frosting, 117
pumpkin cream cheese frosting, 118

Cheese, Parmesan
basil pesto, 87, 88
green eggs & ham, 75
homemade ranch dressing, 218
little Italy meatballs, 197
polpette di sarde, 233
pupperoni pizza pies, 93
roman style tripe, 234
tasty tuna treats, 95
turkey burgers, 204

Cheese, Ricotta
loaves of lamb, 229

Cheese, Swiss
chicken cordon bleu, 69

Cherries
cherry fruit leather, 163
healthy ingredients, 19

Chia Seeds
blueberry chia seed jelly, 114
safe herbs & spices, 30
secret spinach smoothies, 138

Chicken
arroz con pollo, 181
chai chicken strips, 162
chicken barley soup, 187
chicken chompers, 165
chicken cordon bleu, 69
chicken gumbo, 189
chicken n greens, 216
chicken, quinoa & kale, 217
chicken salad, 218
healthy ingredients, 19
hunter's chicken stew, 225
maple cinnamon chicken jerky, 171
southwestern chicken chili, 202
the fabulous frittata, 243
tips & tricks, 264

Chicken Carcass
barkin bird bones, 107
make your own chicken stock, 257

Chicken Gizzards
chicken gizzard casserole, 188
chicken gizzard stew, 214

Chicken Livers
chicken liver meatballs, 215
healthy ingredients, 19
tips & tricks, 264

Chicken Stock
arroz con pollo, 181
barkaritas, 142
bark beer, 132
beef heart soup, 211
canned fish stew, 213
chicken gizzard stew, 214
chicken gumbo, 189
chicken n greens, 216
chicken, quinoa & kale, 217
cinnamon beef stew, 219
greek lamb patties, 193
hunter's chicken stew, 225

kibble gravy, 249
lamb nuggets, 78
liver pate' bites, 81
meaty gummy paws, 124
mighty dog mutt balls, 127
puppermint patties, 92
southwestern chicken chili, 202
turkey n rye meaty bones, 99

Chickpeas
honey roasted chickpeas, 113

Cinnamon
all american apple pie, 103
banana carob frosting, 119
banana carob pupcakes, 54
barkin bacon bites, 56
breakfast porridge, 185
butternut bliss biscuits, 60
carrot pupcakes, 63
chai chicken strips, 162
cinnamon beef stew, 219
cinnamon carob ice cream, 143
coconut catters, 70
did you say bacon? pupsicles, 148
grrreat granola bars, 72
harvest pumpkin balls, 77
honey roasted chickpeas, 113
maple cinnamon chicken jerky, 171
mighty dog mutt balls, 127
pawsome pumpkin pupcakes, 85
power punch, 135
pumpkin cran muffins, 91
pumpkin pie pupsicles, 152
pumpkin please, 251
pumpkin puppucinos, 137
safe herbs & spices, 30
savory turkey muttloaf, 237
thanksgiving dinner, 241
the kirbylicious barkday cake, 98

Coconut
coconut butter, 248
coconut catters, 70

coconut ice cream, 145
grrreat granola bars, 72
healthy ingredients, 19
pumpkin please, 251

Coconut Cream
copycat starbucks puppucino, 133

Coconut Flour
all american apple pie, 103
chicken gizzard stew, 214
chicken liver meatballs, 215
cinnamon beef stew, 219
coconut fish soup, 221
grrreat granola bars, 72
hearty beef stew, 224
safe flours, 36

Coconut Milk
canned fish stew, 213
coconut catters, 70
coconut ice cream, 145
coconut fish soup, 221
copycat starbucks puppucino, 133
decadent pb pupsicles, 147
frosty freezy ice cream, 150
power punch, 135
pumpkin please, 251
savory turkey muttloaf, 237
viva la venison, 205

Coconut Oil
banana carob frosting, 119
banana carob pupcakes, 54
canned fish stew, 213
carob avocado frosting, 119
carob, peanut butter, yogurt chips, 117
chai chicken strips, 162
christmas carob bark, 123
peanut butter cups, 131
savory turkey muttloaf, 237

Coconut Sugar
copycat starbucks puppucino, 133

Cottage Cheese
chicken gumbo, 189
cottage cheese muttins, 191

Cranberries
chicken gizzard casserole, 188
chicken liver meatballs, 215
harmful ingredients, 25
healthy ingredients, 19
mississippi mud puppies, 84
pumpkin cran muffins, 91
thanksgiving dinner, 241
turkey n rye meaty bones, 99

Cucumber
vita veggie mashup, 256

Dill Seed
canned fish stew, 213
champion fish chews, 161
homemade ranch dressing, 218
safe herbs & spices, 31

Eggs
all american apple pie, 103
avocado egg salad, 209
bacon, eggs & quinoa, 210
baked rice cakes, 53
banana carob pupcakes, 54
bananaramas, 55
barkin bacon bites, 56
blueberry pupcakes, 57
butternut bliss biscuits, 60
cajun bacon biscuits, 61
carrot pupcakes, 63
cheeseburgers, 65
chicken cordon bleu, 69
chicken liver meatballs, 215
chicken salad, 218
coconut catters, 70
coconut ice cream, 145
cottage cheese muttins, 191
greek lamb patties, 193
green eggs & ham, 75
harmful ingredients, 27
harvest pumpkin balls, 77
hawaiian burgers, 223
healthy ingredients, 20
holy mackerel, 111
lamb nuggets, 78
little Italy meatballs, 197
liver dumplings, 227
liver lover's meaty bones, 79
liver pate' bites, 81
meaty muffins, 198
milk bones, 83
mississippi mud puppies, 84
monster mashed muttins, 230
muttloaf, 199
pawsome pumpkin pupcakes, 85
pb scrambled eggs, 231
peanut butter paws, 86
pesto puppers, 87
polpette di sarde, 233
pumpkin cran muffins, 91
puppermint patties, 92
pupperoni pizza pies, 93
savory scrambled eggs, 236
scrambled eggs & tuna, 239
shepherd's pie, 201
sweet potato puffs, 94
tasty tuna treats, 95
thanksgiving dinner, 241
the fabulous frittata, 243
the incredible egg, 37
the kirbylicious barkday cake, 98
turkey burgers, 204
turkey n rye meaty bones, 99
viva la venison, 205

Egg Shell, Ground
asian fish balls, 208
arroz con pollo, 181
beef heart soup, 211

beefy kale pasta, 183
breakfast muffins, 212
canned fish stew, 213
chazuke, 186
chicken barley soup, 187
chicken gizzard casserole, 188
chicken gizzard stew, 214
chicken gumbo, 189
chicken liver meatballs, 215
chicken n greens, 216
chicken, quinoa & kale, 217
cinnamon beef stew, 219
coconut fish soup, 221
cottage cheese muttins, 191
country roots beef stew, 222
greek lamb patties, 193
hamburger helper canine style, 195
hawaiian burgers, 223
healthy ingredients, 20
hearty beef stew, 224
hunter's chicken stew, 225
little Italy meatballs, 197
liver dumplings, 227
loaves of lamb, 229
meaty muffins, 198
monster mashed muttins, 230
muttloaf, 199
polpette di sarde, 233
roman style tripe, 234
savory scrambled eggs, 236
savory turkey muttloaf, 237
scrambled eggs & tuna, 239
shepherd's pie, 201
southwestern chicken chili, 202
thanksgiving dinner, 241
the fabulous frittata, 243
the incredible egg, 38
tuna salad, 244
turkey burgers, 204
venison stew, 245
viva la venison, 205

Flax Seed, ground
banana maple crisps, 105
bananaramas, 55

chicken gumbo, 189
grrreat granola bars, 72
harvest pumpkin balls, 77
mighty dog mutt balls, 127
mississippi mud puppies, 84
muttloaf, 199
peanut butter & jelly sandwiches, 114
safe herbs & spices, 31
sweet potato puffs, 94
tips & tricks, 263
turkey n rye meaty bones, 99

Flour, Any
hamburger helper canine style, 195

Fruit, Dried
coconut fish soup, 221
grrreat granola bars, 72

Fruit, frozen
frosty freezy ice cream, 150

Fruit Juice
fruity gummy paws, 125
fruity ice pups, 149
my sweetheart jerky, 172

Garlic (ground, minced)
basil pesto, 87, 88
beef heart soup, 211
beefy kale pasta, 183
canned fish stew, 213
cheeseburgers, 65
chicken barley soup, 187
chicken gumbo, 189
chicken liver meatballs, 215
cinnamon beef stew, 219
coconut fish soup, 221
country roots beef stew, 222
doggie crack aka pig ears, 167
garlic is good, 39
hamburger helper canine style, 195

the canine chef cookbook

---

hearty beef stew, 224
homemade ranch dressing, 218
hunter's chicken stew, 225
kibble gravy, 249
little Italy meatballs, 197
liver dumplings, 227
loaves of lamb, 229
make your own bone broth, 258
my sweetheart jerky, 172
oh my deer jerky, 173
polpette di sarde, 233
roman style tripe, 234
safe herbs & spices, 31
savory turkey muttloaf, 237
shepherd's pie, 201
southwestern chicken chili, 202
venison stew, 245
viva la venison, 205

Gelatin
banana lemon gummy paws, 124
fruity gummy paws, 125
healthy ingredients, 20
meaty gummy paws, 124

Ginger
canned fish stew, 213
chai chicken strips , 162
chazuke, 186
chicken gumbo, 189
coconut fish soup, 221
greek lamb patties, 193
grrreat granola bars, 72
hawaiian burgers, 223
my sweetheart jerky, 172
pawsome pumpkin pupcakes, 85
pumpkin cran muffins, 91
pumpkin please, 251
pumpkin puppucinos, 137
safe herbs & spices, 31
savory turkey muttloaf, 237

Green Beans
chicken gumbo, 189
healthy ingredients, 20

shepherd's pie, 201
thanksgiving dinner, 241
vita veggie mashup, 256

Green Tea
Chazuke, 186
power punch, 135
safe herbs & spices, 31
secret spinach smoothies, 138

Ham
green eggs & ham, 75
the kirbylicious barkday cake, 98

Ham Bouillon
doggie crack aka pig ears, 167

Herring
baked rice cakes, 53
healthy ingredients, 20

Honey
all american apple pie, 103
bacon cream cheese frosting, 118
blueberry chia seed jelly, 114
carrot pupcakes, 63
cherry fruit leather, 163
coconut catters, 70
cream cheese frosting, 117
harvest pumpkin balls, 77
healthy ingredients, 20
honey roasted chickpeas, 113
mighty dog mutt balls, 127
patriotic pupsicles, 151
pawsome pumpkin pupcakes, 85
peanut butter, 250
pumpkin cran muffins, 91
pumpkin please, 251
pumpkin puppucinos, 137
secret spinach smoothies, 138
tips & tricks, 263

Honeycomb Tripe
roman style tripe, 234

Kale
beefy kale pasta, 183
chicken, quinoa & kale, 217
cinnamon beef stew, 219
healthy ingredients, 20
vita veggie mashup, 256

Kefir
strawberry kefir milkshake, 139

Kelp
baked rice cakes, 53
chazuke, 186
healthy ingredients, 19
safe herbs & spices, 31

Kiwi
secret spinach smoothies, 138

Lamb
greek lamb patties, 193
healthy ingredients, 20
lamb nuggets, 78
loaves of lamb, 229

Lamb Broth
greek lamb patties, 193

Lemon Juice
avocado egg salad, 209
banana lemon gummy paws, 124
basil pesto, 87, 88
champion fish chews, 161
holy mackerel, 111

Lentils
chicken gumbo, 189

Liver, Calf
healthy ingredients, 21
liver dumplings, 227
liver lover's meaty bones, 79
liver pate' bites, 81
love some liver jerky, 169
mississippi mud puppies, 84
tips & tricks, 264
twice as good beef jerky, 177

Mackerel
baked rice cakes, 53
canned fish stew, 213
holy mackerel, 111

Maple Syrup
bacon cream cheese frosting, 118
banana maple crisps, 105
butternut bliss biscuits, 60
carob avocado frosting, 119
cream cheese frosting, 117
did you say bacon? Pupsicles, 148
healthy ingredients, 21
maple cinnamon chicken jerky, 171
maple frosting, 116
peanut butter & jelly sandwiches, 114
pumpkin please, 251
pumpkin puppucinos, 137
the kirbylicious barkday cake, 98

Milk
did you say bacon? pupsicles, 148
hamburger helper canine style, 195
healthy ingredients, 21
mashed potato frosting, 120
pb pill pockets, 129
yogurt frosting, 116

Milk (dry)
Bananaramas, 55
cajun bacon biscuits, 61
lamb nuggets, 78
milk bones, 83

peanut butter paws, 86
puppermint patties, 92
turkey n rye meaty bones, 99

Mint
christmas carob bark, 123
hunter's chicken stew, 225
loaves of lamb, 229
puppermint patties, 92
roman style tripe, 234
safe herbs & spices, 32

Molasses (blackstrap)
Cheeseburgers, 65
coconut ice cream, 145
grrreat granola bars, 72
harvest pumpkin balls, 77
healthy ingredients, 21
peanut butter paws, 86
sweet potato chews, 174

Oat Flour
Bananaramas, 55
barkin bacon bites, 56
blueberry pupcakes, 57
butternut bliss biscuits, 60
carrot pupcakes, 63
chicken cordon bleu, 69
coconut catters, 70
ezy cheesy, 71
harvest pumpkin balls, 77
liver lover's meaty bones, 79
mississippi mud puppies, 84
pawsome pumpkin pupcakes, 85
peanut butter paws, 86
pesto puppers, 87
pumpkin cran muffins, 91
puppermint patties, 92
safe flours, 35
tasty tuna treats, 95
the kirbylicious barkday cake, 98
tips & tricks, 264

Oats
b'oat bites, 58
breakfast porridge, 185
grrreat granola bars, 72
healthy ingredients, 21
meaty muffins, 198
muttloaf, 199
soak those grains, 43
thanksgiving dinner, 241
viva la venison, 205

Olive Oil
basil pesto , 87, 88
beef heart soup, 211
champion fish chews, 161
chicken barley soup, 187
chicken cordon bleu, 69
chicken gizzard stew, 214
chicken liver meatballs, 215
country roots beef stew, 222
green eggs & ham, 75
healthy ingredients, 21
hearty beef stew, 224
homemade ranch dressing, 218
honey roasted chickpeas, 113
hunter's chicken stew, 225
liver pate' bites, 81
loaves of lamb, 229
meaty muffins, 198
roasted baby carrots, 253
roasted sweet potatoes, 255
roman style tripe, 234
savory beef bits, 115
scrambled eggs & tuna, 239
the kirbylicious barkday cake, 98
turkey jerky, 175
turkey n rye meaty bones, 99
venison stew, 245
viva la venison, 205

Oregano
country roots beef stew, 222
pupperoni pizza pies, 93
safe herbs & spices, 32

Organ Meat
    barkin bird bones, 107

Parsley
    asian fish balls, 208
    arroz con pollo, 181
    avocado egg salad, 209
    champion fish chews, 161
    chicken barley soup, 187
    chicken chompers, 165
    chicken gumbo, 189
    chicken liver meatballs, 215
    country roots beef stew, 222
    hamburger helper canine style, 195
    holy mackerel , 111
    hunter's chicken stew, 225
    lamb nuggets, 78
    little italy meatballs, 197
    liver pate' bites, 81
    loaves of lamb, 229
    make your own bone broth, 258
    mashed potato frosting, 120
    muttloaf, 199
    polpette di sarde, 233
    puppermint patties, 92
    pupperoni pizza pies, 93
    safe herbs & spices, 32
    savory beef bits, 115
    shepherd's pie, 201
    southwestern chicken chili, 202
    thanksgiving dinner, 241
    turkey n rye meaty bones, 99
    venison stew, 245
    viva la venison, 205

Pasta
    beefy kale pasta, 183
    cinnamon beef stew, 219
    hamburger helper canine style, 195

Peaches
    b'oat bites, 58

Peanut Butter
    carob, peanut butter, yogurt chips, 117
    decadent pb pupsicles, 147
    grrreat granola bars, 72
    healthy ingredients, 21
    mighty dog mutt balls, 127
    pb pill pockets, 129
    pb scrambled eggs, 231
    peanut butter & jelly sandwiches, 114
    peanut butter cups, 131
    peanut butter paws, 86
    tasty tuna treats, 95

Peanuts
    peanut butter, 250

Pears
    healthy ingredients, 21
    sardine parfait, 235

Pepperoni
    pupperoni pizza pies, 93

Peppers (Red, Green)
    beefy kale pasta, 183
    chicken barley soup, 187
    chicken liver meatballs, 215
    hunter's chicken stew, 225
    loaves of lamb, 229
    roman style tripe, 234
    vita veggie mashup, 256

Pig Ears
    doggie crack aka pig ears, 167

Pineapple (canned, dried)
    breakfast porridge, 185
    hawaiian burgers, 223

Pork
    hawaiian burgers, 223

Potato Flakes
    cheesy mashed taters, 109
    holy mackerel, 111
    meaty muffins, 198
    monster mashed muttins, 230
    polpette di sarde, 233
    thanksgiving dinner, 241

Potato Flour
    lamb nuggets, 78
    safe flours, 36

Potatoes
    country roots beef stew, 222
    healthy ingredients, 22
    hearty beef stew, 224
    mashed potato frosting, 120
    meaty muffins, 198
    shepherd's pie, 201
    the carnivore's cake, 203
    venison stew, 245

Pumpkin
    b'oat bites, 58
    breakfast porridge, 185
    chicken gizzard casserole, 188
    harvest pumpkin balls, 77
    healthy ingredients, 22
    pawsome pumpkin pupcakes, 85
    pumpkin cran muffins, 91
    pumpkin cream cheese frosting, 118
    pumpkin pie pupsicles, 152
    pumpkin please, 251
    pumpkin puppucinos, 137
    thanksgiving dinner, 241
    the great plumpkin, 97

Quinoa
    bacon, eggs & quinoa, 210
    chicken, quinoa & kale, 217
    healthy ingredients, 22
    mighty dog mutt balls, 127

Rice
    baked rice cakes, 53
    chazuke, 186

Rice Flour
    pesto puppers, 87
    sweet potato puffs, 94

Rosemary
    chicken chompers, 165
    chicken gumbo, 189
    cinnamon beef stew, 219
    greek lamb patties, 193
    hearty beef stew, 224
    lamb nuggets, 78
    safe herbs & spices, 32
    thanksgiving dinner, 241
    venison stew, 245

Rye Flour
    cajun bacon biscuits, 61
    healthy ingredients, 22
    pupperoni pizza pies, 93
    safe flours, 35
    turkey n rye meaty bones, 99

Safflower Oil
    blueberry pupcakes, 57
    chicken gizzard casserole, 188
    healthy ingredients, 22
    pawsome pumpkin pupcakes, 85

Salmon
    canned fish stew, 213
    chazuke, 186
    healthy ingredients, 22

the canine chef cookbook

Salmon Oil
    healthy ingredients, 22
    tasty tuna treats, 95

Sardines
    healthy ingredients, 22
    little italy meatballs, 197
    polpette di sarde, 233
    sardine parfait, 235

Sausage (pork, turkey)
    breakfast muffins, 212

Sea Salt
    all american apple pie, 103
    asian fish balls, 208
    avocado egg salad, 209
    baked rice cakes, 53
    banana carob pupcakes, 54
    bananaramas, 55
    basil pesto, 87, 88
    beef heart soup, 211
    beefy kale pasta, 183
    butternut bliss biscuits, 60
    chazuke, 186
    cheeseburgers, 65
    cheese nips kinda, 67
    cheesy mashed taters, 109
    chicken barley soup, 187
    chicken cordon bleu, 69
    chicken gumbo, 189
    chicken liver meatballs, 215
    chicken n greens, 216
    cinnamon beef stew, 219
    country roots beef stew, 222
    doggie crack aka pig ears, 167
    green eggs & ham, 75
    grrreat granola bars, 72
    hamburger helper canine style, 195
    harmful ingredients, 27
    harvest pumpkin balls, 77
    hearty beef stew, 224
    holy mackerel, 111
    honey roasted chickpeas, 113
    kibble gravy, 249
    little italy meatballs, 197
    liver dumplings, 227
    make your own bone broth, 258
    meaty muffins, 198
    mighty dog mutt balls, 127
    milk bones, 83
    pawsome pumpkin pupcakes, 85
    pb scrambled eggs, 231
    peanut butter, 250
    pesto puppers, 87
    polpette di sarde, 233
    roasted baby carrots, 253
    roasted sweet potatoes, 255
    safe herbs & spices, 32
    savory turkey muttloaf, 237
    shepherd's pie, 201
    southwestern chicken chili, 202
    thanksgiving dinner, 241
    the fabulous frittata, 243
    venison stew, 245
    viva la venison, 205

Spelt Flour
    healthy ingredients, 22
    safe flours, 35
    tasty tuna treats, 95

Spinach
    bark beer, 132
    breakfast muffins, 212
    chicken gizzard casserole, 188
    chicken liver meatballs, 215
    green eggs & ham, 75
    healthy ingredients, 22
    savory turkey muttloaf, 237
    secret spinach smoothies, 138
    the fabulous frittata, 243

Squash
    beef heart soup, 211
    butternut bliss biscuits, 60
    chicken gumbo, 189
    healthy ingredients, 23

hearty beef stew, 224
loaves of lamb, 229
vita veggie mashup, 256

Strawberries
patriotic pupsicles, 151
strawberry kefir milkshake, 139

Sweet Peas
canned fish stew, 213
coconut fish soup, 221
healthy ingredients, 21

Sweet Potato/Yam
beef heart soup, 211
canned fish stew, 213
coconut fish soup, 221
cottage cheese muttins, 191
healthy ingredients, 23
roasted sweet potatoes, 255
safe flours, 36
sweet potato chews, 174
sweet potato puffs, 94
thanksgiving dinner, 241
venison stew, 245

Tapioca Starch
maple frosting, 116
yogurt frosting, 116

Thyme
cinnamon beef stew, 219
safe herbs & spices, 33

Tilapia
champion fish chews, 161

Tomatoes (fresh, dried, juice)
cinnamon beef stew, 219
country roots beef stew, 222

harmful ingredients, 26
healthy ingredients, 23
hunter's chicken stew, 225
loaves of lamb, 229
muttloaf, 199
roman style tripe, 234
the fabulous frittata, 243
turkey burgers, 204

Tomatoes, paste
cinnamon beef stew, 219
pupperoni pizza pies, 93

Tuna Fish
healthy ingredients, 23
scrambled eggs & tuna, 239
tasty tuna treats, 95
tuna salad, 244

Turkey
healthy ingredients, 23
little italy meatballs, 197
savory turkey muttloaf, 237
thanksgiving dinner, 241
turkey burgers, 204
turkey jerky, 175
turkey n rye meaty bones, 99

Turmeric
asian fish balls, 208
avocado egg salad, 209
beef heart soup, 211
chicken gumbo, 189
chicken n greens, 216
greek lamb patties, 193
safe herbs & spices, 33
savory turkey muttloaf, 237
thanksgiving dinner, 241

Turnips, Turnip Greens
beef heart soup, 211
chicken n greens, 216

the canine chef cookbook

country roots beef stew, 222
healthy ingredients, 23

Vanilla Extract
all american apple pie, 103
banana carob frosting, 119
banana carob pupcakes, 54
bananaramas, 55
blueberry pupcakes, 57
butternut bliss biscuits, 60
cherry fruit leather, 163
coconut ice cream, 145
copycat starbucks puppucino, 133
grrreat granola bars, 72
pawsome pumpkin pupcakes, 85
pesto puppers, 87
pumpkin please, 251
pumpkin puppucinos, 137
roman style tripe, 234

Vegetables, Mixed
chicken gizzard stew, 214
hamburger helper canine style, 195
make your own chicken stock, 257

Venison
healthy ingredients, 23
oh my deer jerky, 173
venison stew, 245
viva la venison, 205

Vinegar (Apple Cider, White)
make your own bone broth, 258
my sweetheart jerky, 172
roman style tripe, 234

Whole Wheat Flour
banana carob frosting, 119
banana carob pupcakes, 54
cheeseburgers, 65
cheese nips kinda, 67
ezy cheesy, 71

milk bones, 83
pupperoni pizza pies, 93
safe flours, 35
tasty tuna treats, 95

Yogurt, Greek
avocado egg salad, 209
banana carob pupcakes, 54
blueberry pupcakes, 57
carob, peanut butter, yogurt chips, 117
carrot pupcakes, 63
cheesy mashed taters, 109
decadent pb popsicles, 147
did you say bacon? pupsicles, 148
greek lamb patties, 193
hamburger helper canine style, 195
healthy ingredients, 23
homemade ranch dressing, 218
patriotic pupsicles, 151
pesto puppers, 87
pumpkin pie pupsicles, 152
pumpkin puppucinos, 137
savory scrambled eggs, 236
the great plumpkin, 97
yogurt frosting, 116
yogurt melt, 154

CPSIA information can be obtained
at www.ICGtesting.com
Printed in the USA
LVHW061929061218
599464LV00007B/46/P